Captain Benjamin Bonneville's

WYOMING EXPEDITION

· THE LOST 1833 REPORT ·

To Bob & Rosanne

Jett

Jett B. Conner

THE
History
PRESS

Published by The History Press
Charleston, SC
www.historypress.com

Front cover, top left: Walters Art Museum. Wikimedia Commons; *top center*: Missouri Historical Society. Wikimedia Commons; *top right*: White House Art Collection, Washington, D.C. Wikimedia Commons; *bottom*: Walters Art Museum. Wikimedia Commons.
Back cover, top: Carol M. Highsmith Archive. Library of Congress; *bottom*: Walters Art Museum. Wikimedia Commons.

First published 2021

Manufactured in the United States

ISBN 9781467148641

Library of Congress Control Number: 2020951824

Notice: The information in this book is true and complete to the best of our knowledge. It is offered without guarantee on the part of the author or The History Press. The author and The History Press disclaim all liability in connection with the use of this book.

For Rosemary

CONTENTS

ACKNOWLEDGEMENTS

I wish to thank Artie Crisp, senior acquisitions editor at The History Press, for his expert assistance with this publication. His good cheer and timely help made it much easier to pull together this book. I also wish to thank my good friend and colleague Steven J. Leonard, former longtime chair of the Department of History at Metropolitan State University of Denver and coauthor of *Colorado: A History of the Centennial State*, for his encouragement with this effort, my first, to write something about the Rocky Mountain West.

MAPS

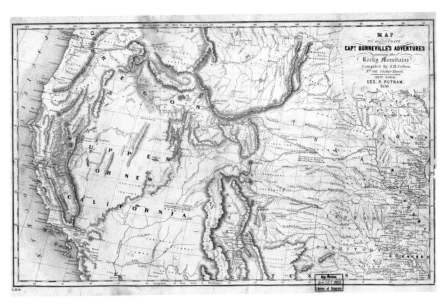

Map to illustrate Captain. Bonneville's adventures among the Rocky Mountains, 1850.
Library of Congress.

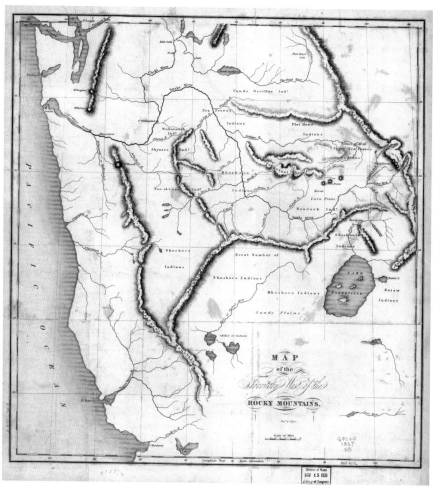

Bonneville's map of the territory west of the Rocky Mountains, 1837. *Library of Congress.*

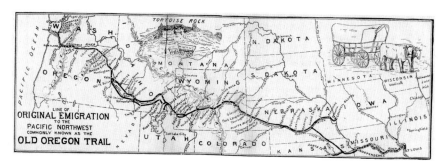

Old Oregon Trail, map print from *The Ox Team or the Old Oregon Trail 1852–1906*, by Ezra Meeker. *Wikimedia Commons.*

INTRODUCTION

Everybody went west. Fur traders and missionaries, Santa Fe merchants and the military, emigrants to Oregon and California poured year after year over the great plains.
—*John Francis McDermott, introduction to* Prairie and Mountain Sketches *by Matthew C. Field*

The era of the Rocky Mountain fur trade, a period of fifteen years from 1825 to 1840, has been variously characterized by historians of the American West as glorious, romantic, golden, a heyday or some other such celebratory description.[1] But just as easily it can also be portrayed as a perilous, daring, confrontational or even dark period of adventurism beyond America's frontier. It all depends on who's doing the describing.

For one thing, many Native Americans in the Rocky Mountains and beyond found little to praise about the fur trade and instead much to resent and resist. The movement of migrants toward today's Oregon, Utah and California that followed a few decades later was made much easier by the mountain men who opened the pathways for future travelers and settlers. But that also eventually led to inevitable clashes with native people, who would have to be defeated, subdued or pushed out of the way. Or simply disappear.

For another thing, competition among the trappers and fur-trading companies, such as the British Hudson's Bay Company, the American Fur Company (founded by John Jacob Astor) and the Rocky Mountain Fur

Company, was fierce and relentless, especially in the Oregon Territory, a region jointly occupied and contested by the United States and Great Britain. Fur traders even accused rival companies of engaging the natives to attack their brigades of trappers. And though the mountain men somehow found a way to coexist and continue operating against a background of declining beaver populations and fewer packs of furs to deliver downstream to depots, their enterprise nevertheless would prove unsustainable.

Caused mostly by overtrapping, the shortage of product and rising costs plagued all competitors, even if retail prices for furs remained relatively steady in the East throughout the era. Of course, changes in fashion—the growing popularity of silk hats and the use of other materials—affected the trade. And undiminished hostilities in the Rocky Mountain West against the mountain men, especially at the hands of the Blackfeet, and too many competitors willing to take the risk anyway to head into the same overworked territories to trap and trade, also contributed to the demise of the business. So, while the early years of the fur trade were brimming with dreams of riches, rarely found, inevitably, they were replaced by years of increasing economic challenges. Of the mountain men who survived it all and managed to come home, most returned with only their memories. Finally, the era came to an end.

Call the period what you may, it was an exciting time of American exploration and discovery, one that fired the imaginations of a population back east hungry to read anything and everything about the mysterious Rockies and western country. It left a trail of names and tales of mountain men and their daring-do whose exploits and stories delivered what readers were lusting for. And many of their wild stories were even true. Names such as William Ashley, Thomas Fitzpatrick, Jedediah Strong Smith, Joseph Rutherford Walker, James "Jim" Bridger, Nathaniel Jarvis Wyeth, William Drummond Stewart, brothers William and Milton Sublette, Robert Campbell and earlier explorers probing the interior of the Rockies such as the intrepid John Colter were recognized in the East for what these men did in the West.

Add to those names another, that of explorer and soldier Captain Benjamin Bonneville. It was his demonstration that a wagon train could roll over the Continental Divide on the Oregon Trail, at South Pass in the southern end of Wyoming's long Wind River Range, that helped shape the beginning of a new era, the era of westward expansion.

This brief history focuses on stories and observations recorded by Captain Bonneville during his first year of adventures in Wyoming and beyond that

One of Alfred Jacob Miller's murals depicting western trappers and "Mountain Men" inside the Jackson Lake Lodge in Grand Teton National Park. *Carol M. Highsmith Archive. Library of Congress.*

lasted for another two and a half years. A career army officer, Bonneville figured out a way to obtain a furlough, go to the Rockies and satisfy much more than his curiosity about western America. He liked it enough to overstay his leave, seemingly unconcerned at the time by the potential consequences of cutting short a promising military career.

His real purposes there have been debated ever since. Just what was he really doing out there in the first place? Though Bonneville's explorations were not particularly remarkable otherwise, he did make his mark in Wyoming and beyond in several notable ways that would have lasting consequences for the future of American migration and expansionism. But without the efforts of a famous American writer, Bonneville's western adventures might not have been noticed or remembered, perhaps earning him only a footnote in the annals of the American West.

In 1837, Washington Irving popularized Bonneville's 1832–35 expedition to the American frontier and far West in his romanticized account *The Adventures of Captain Bonneville* (originally published as *Rocky Mountains: Scenes, Incidents and Adventures in the Far West*). Irving met Bonneville in 1835 and purchased Bonneville's manuscript and materials from his expedition for $1,000, after Bonneville could not find a publisher willing to buy his story about his travels. Irving used Bonneville's material as the basis for a third story he wrote and added to two others already completed to make a trilogy of tales, which appears today as *Three Western Narratives: A Tour on the Prairies,*

Left: General Benjamin L.E. Bonneville, photograph. *Missouri Historical Society. Wikimedia Commons.*

Right: Washington Irving, photograph by M.C. Brady. *Library of Congress.*

Astoria, The Adventures of Captain Bonneville.[2] Irving's story was so successful it created a brand for the name *Bonneville*.

Today, that name most likely evokes the eponymous Bonneville Salt Flats in Utah (B-Ville Flats to racing fans), where speed records are set by land rockets and all sorts of piston-driven wheeled contrivances. But the name has also been bestowed on an American automobile (now extinct), a British motorcycle (the third iteration), a power dam, a Pleistocene lake (also extinct), a county, a town, a mountain peak and even a crater on Mars, among other things. Benjamin Bonneville would be pleased. He also put his name on the Great Salt Lake on the maps he drew, even though he never actually saw its waters. But that didn't stick. Only much later would it be realized that the Great Salt Lake is a remnant of a much larger paleo-lake that was twenty thousand square miles in size. This lake was named Bonneville in his honor. It would surely amuse him to know that his name is finally associated with the Great Salt Lake after all.

In addition to maps, Bonneville brought back from his expedition a record of his adventures. It should be noted that there were several manuscripts from Bonneville's expedition: the original journal Bonneville submitted to the U.S. Army on his return from the Rockies in 1835 (he called it a diary as well as a journal) and the materials Irving purchased. Both have since disappeared. Irving adapted two maps from Bonneville's original journal that he had copied directly from the Department of the Army for use in the early editions of his book. He stated that he saw the journal in September 1835:

> *Capt. Bonneville, who has recently returned from the Rocky Mountains has had the kindness to show me his journal in which are a few small maps of various parts of those mountains. As these maps throw a light on the topography of certain portions of the country about which I feel some curiosity I am desirous of getting copies of two or three of them. Capt. Bonneville tells me it is possible the journal may be separated in your Department. If so I should take it as a great favor if you would have copied for me the map of the Wind River Mountains, and another containing Henry Fort and the upper branches of Snake River. There are two other maps illustrating the course of Snake river which I should likewise have, I ask these copies on the presumption that there will be no objection on the part of the department to have them copied, and perhaps published. Any expense incurred by their being copied I shall gladly repay.*[3]

The journal was not the only important document of Bonneville's that was lost. In the 1920s, researchers rummaging through military files and searching for Bonneville materials in Washington, D.C., rediscovered a treasure-trove of old documents, one in particular that mattered greatly to the army career of Captain Bonneville.[4] It was a report in the form of a letter he sent to the commanding officer of the United States Army, Major General Alexander Macomb, informing him of his intentions to extend his one-year leave while continuing to explore in the Rocky Mountain West and beyond, unless he heard otherwise. He knew, of course, that it would take a year to get a reply back to him. But the report he sent back east in 1833, though received, was misplaced and perhaps never even read. In the meantime, Bonneville continued his fur-trading expedition for another year.

But the loss of the report proved problematic for Bonneville. He assumed, after the report's carrier, mountain man Michael Cerre, returned to Bonneville's camp a year later from the East and reported that Bonneville's request for an extended leave was supported, that he had permission to continue his explorations. He did not, as he would eventually learn. By the time Bonneville returned to the States in 1835, he found that he had been bounced out of the military and, worse, was thought to be dead. It took the adventurer almost a year, with the help of President Andrew Jackson, to return to his old regiment and rank.

Unlike whatever manuscript materials Irving bought from Bonneville at the end of his expedition, and the original journal Bonneville submitted to the army, his report to Macomb, sometimes called "the lost report," was finally located. It is a report that Irving did not have access to when writing *The Adventures of Captain Bonneville*; nor did western historian Hiram M. Chittenden when he wrote his well-known *The American Fur Trade of the Far West*. Chittenden's chapter on Bonneville relied heavily on Irving's account.[5] But Bonneville's lost report adds to the story of his adventures in the West.

The report delivered to Macomb provides firsthand details of Bonneville's first year in the heart of the Rocky Mountains, written by the soldier-explorer himself. And it adds some intrigue to the questions, long raised by historians and biographers, about what exactly he was doing for the U.S. government while on his unpaid leave and privately funded expedition, publicly billed as a fur-trading expedition. Was he really just leading such an expedition? Was he trying to get rich? Was he sent by the U.S. Army to do reconnaissance in the disputed lands of the far West, as has often been speculated since? Or was he simply having an adventure of a lifetime? As will be seen, the rediscovered lost report and related letters provide several clues.

Moreover, questions have been raised over the years about Irving's tales of western expeditions. Due to his flourishes and storytelling style— especially by mixing in details from his own experiences and hearsay— and his reputation as a writer of fiction (*The Legend of Sleepy Hollow*, *Rip Van Winkle*), doubts surfaced long ago about whether Irving's accounts were based on fact. He never, for example, visited Astoria, even though he wrote a book about it. But in a 1964 edition of Irving's *Astoria*, editor Edgeley W. Todd included a synopsis dispelling the notion that Irving's work was not reliable. He concluded that Irving's stories were rooted in a large number of documents, including firsthand accounts, and that the Astoria story was a faithful rendering of tales told.[6]

Although Bonneville's original journal and materials have never been found, his firsthand descriptions of Wyoming and the Rocky Mountain West do exist, along with several maps of the region, based on Irving's work and Bonneville's report and surviving letters. And, except for a few instances noted in this book where dates and directions sometimes get crossed up, Irving's and Bonneville's accounts of the captain's first year in the Rockies reliably correlate. But, because Irving did not have Bonneville's missing report to the military when he wrote his story about the soldier's adventures, he may not have been able to fully address the question of Bonneville's purported military purpose in exploring the Rocky Mountains and beyond. Or maybe he knew more and simply chose not to do so.

A reprint of the lost report of 1833 (called the Report hereafter in this book) may be found in the appendix, along with other relevant letters rediscovered in the 1920s. These materials help add to the story of Bonneville's adventures in Wyoming and beyond the Rocky Mountains.

1

A JOURNEY BEGINS

On the day of departure at Fort Osage overlooking the Missouri River, a tingle of excitement ran through the crowd. Maybe it was because this was the first time anyone had organized a wagon train to cross the Continental Divide in Wyoming's Rocky Mountains. Though not the first time wagons went into the region, this was not the mode of transportation used by fur traders intending to reach a rendezvous west of the Rockies. Maybe it was the unusual entourage of 121 adventurers that the expedition leader Captain Bonneville had assembled, including Americans, French and several members of the Delaware tribe, plus horses, mules, cattle and twenty wagons. And maybe it was just because any departure to the fabled far West at that time was somewhat akin to watching people leave for the moon.

An excursion to the Rockies bestowed on participants a certain charisma. As Washington Irving described trappers and fur traders, the "mountaineers" were the western explorers of the 1830s, as distinguished from the canoe and bateaux voyagers of earlier northern and western fur-trading operations:

> *The* ["French" are] *meant to designate the French Creole of Canada or Louisiana; the* ["Americans"], *the trapper of the old American stock, from Kentucky, Tennessee, and others of the western states. The French trapper is represented as a lighter, softer, more self-indulgent kind of man. He must have his Indian wife, his lodge, and his petty conveniences. He is gay and thoughtless, takes little heed of landmarks, depends upon his leaders and companions to think for the common weal, and, if left to himself, is easily perplexed and lost....The American trapper stands by himself and is*

Trappers, watercolor by Alfred Jacob Miller. *Walters Art Museum. Wikimedia Commons.*

peerless for the service of the wilderness. Drop him in the midst of a prairie, or in the heart of the mountains, and he is never at a loss. He notices every landmark; can retrace his route through the most monotonous plains, or the most perplexed labyrinths of the mountains; no danger nor difficulty can appall him, and he scorns to complain under any privation.[7]

The Trapper and His Family, painting by Charles Deas. *Museum of Fine Arts, Boston. Wikimedia Commons.*

Captain Bonneville employed two sub-leaders of his convoy who likely served as models for Washington Irving's stereotypes and biases: Joseph Rutherford Walker and Michael (Michel Silvestre) Cerre. Both were experienced mountaineers, having explored, trapped and traded extensively in the lands west of the Rockies. Walker (rendered by Irving as I.R. Walker, probably because he mistook Bonneville's handwriting), hailed indeed from Tennessee. He had lived for years in Missouri, on the frontier, and had been an early traveler to Santa Fe, where he was arrested and held captive for a time by the authorities in the Mexican Territory. Cerre, son and grandson of French Canadian fur traders, was from St. Louis. He too had been to Santa Fe, endured hardships there and at the young age of twenty-five already was an experienced Indian trader. Both played major roles in the Bonneville expedition to the Rockies and beyond. And as this book will show, Bonneville and Walker shared one odd trait about this upcoming fur-trading expedition: neither was particularly interested in trapping beaver. Both had wider interests in the American West.

For his part, Bonneville was a Frenchman who grew up in the United States. He was no mountaineer, at least not yet. By the time he organized his expedition, he had gained experience on the edge of the American frontier while stationed in the Arkansas and Oklahoma Territories, surveying the lands and negotiating with native people. So, he was no neophyte on the American plains west of the Missouri. But he would be a newcomer to the Rocky Mountain West.

Born Benjamin Louis Eulalie Bonneville in 1796 in Evreux, Normandy, Bonneville spent the first seven years of his childhood growing up in the aftermath of the French Revolution. Biographer Edith Lovell pointed out that Bonneville's name was "indicative of the muddled loyalties of the times," as the name *Benjamin* was given after Benjamin Franklin, and *Louis* was after the late king of France."[8] In the year of Bonneville's birth, France was at war with Austria, and a young army officer named Napoleon Bonaparte was beginning to distinguish himself on the battlefields for the French army.[9]

The French Revolution, begun in 1789, was not complete. Following the storming of the Bastille and the arrest and eventual beheading of King Louis XVI, the revolution had dissolved into a desperate struggle for power among the moderate and radical revolutionary factions and leaders, culminating in the ascendency of the radical leader Maximilien Robespierre and the bloody Reign of Terror. Many leading figures of the moderate revolutionary factions, political and literary, were guillotined before the Terror turned upon itself for more blood.

Benjamin was born two years after Robespierre was arrested by moderates of the ruling French Directory. After a trial, Robespierre met his own fate at the guillotine, ending the Terror. Benjamin's father, Nicholas, was a printer, translator and publisher of revolutionary materials, including Thomas Paine's *Rights of Man*. Benjamin's mother, Marguerite Brazier, was a merchant and writer. Though imprisoned for a time along with other moderates during the Terror, Nicholas escaped execution.

Paine, the famous writer of *Common Sense* and *The American Crisis*, left for Europe just before the American Constitutional Convention in 1787, shuttling back and forth between England and France while seeking patents for an iron bridge he had invented and hoping to find the funds to build it. But he got caught up in both countries' radical movements, which he famously promoted in two volumes of his *Rights of Man*. Escaping from England to France before British authorities could arrest him after charges of sedition were leveled following publication of the second volume of his new work, Paine became more directly involved in French revolutionary affairs. He was elected a delegate to the National Convention as a Girondist and imprisoned during the Terror. He barely avoided being sent to the guillotine.

Thomas Paine, portrait by Laurent Dabos. *National Portrait Gallery, Washington, D.C.*

According to a story often repeated, the door to Paine's cell was open one evening in the Luxembourg Prison in Paris when the jailer came by marking an *X* on the doors of those to be tried and sent to the guillotine the next day. Then it was closed with the *X* inside by the time the jailers came by in the morning to escort those chosen to meet their fate. This story, or some variation of it, has been passed down by most historians and biographers. As one scholar has recently argued, however, the story is without confirmation.[10] Still, here is what Paine said about it:

> *The room in which I was lodged was on the ground floor, and one of a long range of rooms under a gallery, and the door of it opened outward and flat against the wall; so that when it was open the inside of the door appeared outward, and the contrary when it was shut. I had three comrades, fellow prisoners with me, Joseph Vanhuele of Bruges, since president of the municipality of that town, Michael Robbins and Bastini of Louvain. When persons by scores and by hundreds were to be taken out of the prison for the Guillotine it was always done in the night, and those who performed that office had a private mark or signal by which they knew what rooms to go to, and what number to take. We, as I have stated, were four, and the door of our room was marked, unobserved by us, with that number in chalk; but it happened, if happening is a proper word, that the mark was put on when the door was open, and flat against the wall, and thereby came on the inside when we shut it at night, and the destroying angel passed by it. A few days after this, Robespierre fell and Mr. Monroe arrived and reclaimed me, and invited me to his house.*[11]

Following his release from prison, and after recuperating with an old American Revolutionary friend and future president, James Monroe, and his wife in their residence in Paris, Paine lived for several years with the Bonneville family on the outskirts of the city. He urged them to immigrate to America. Nicholas, who became a critic of Napoleon after he rose to power and got in trouble with the new regime as a result, was reluctant to leave his affairs after his business had been seized and he was briefly imprisoned by authorities. In 1802, Paine returned to America at the urging of President Thomas Jefferson, another old Revolution friend. Very soon after, Marguerite and her two boys, Benjamin and Thomas, Paine's godson, accepted Paine's invitation and sailed for the United States. Nicholas stayed behind. Benjamin was eight years old when he arrived in his new country. In America, Marguerite would become Margaret.

Madame Bonneville served as Paine's caretaker in his later years as his health began to fail. He had paid for her rent and upkeep since her arrival to America, though he often groused about the arrangement (and costs). Her two boys were his wards, and he was fond of them. It should be noted that some writers think that there were three boys who accompanied their mother to America: Louis, Benjamin and Thomas. But there is no evidence that a third boy named Louis was with them. He likely died in France as a young child, and a sister may have as well. Paine only mentioned Bebia (Paine's nickname for Benjamin) and Thomas in his correspondence after his return to America.[12] He never spoke of Louis.

Thomas Paine died in New York City in 1809, a famous writer who by then had become infamous in America for two chief reasons. One, he was a freethinker and deist who attacked all organized and revealed religion, including Christianity, in his theistic work, *Age of Reason*. He wrote the work while imprisoned in Paris and managed to smuggle it out during the Terror. The publication alienated many Americans, including old Revolution friends such as Samuel Adams and Dr. Benjamin Rush. And it angered many others. Once, an attempt was made on his life when someone shot through a window at his cottage on his farm in New Rochelle, a confiscated Tory property given to Paine by the New York legislature as compensation for his contributions to the American Revolution.

Two, he attacked President George Washington in an open letter written after Paine's imprisonment in France, accusing him of doing nothing to

Thomas Paine's Cottage in New Rochelle, New York. A portion of this home, which was relocated from his farm, is original. *Photo by author.*

help him get out of prison. The American envoy to Paris, Monroe, helped him get released following the death of Robespierre by convincing French authorities that Paine was an American citizen. He warned Paine not to publish his vindictive letter, but he did anyway. At the time Paine was seeking his release, Washington was engaged in sensitive negotiations with the English while the Treaty of London was being developed, a treaty that was not favorable to the French government. Paine's revolutionary activities and imprisonment in France may have been a touchy subject for the French (and therefore for President Washington), while the Americans were negotiating favorable trade status with the British. In any case, after publication of his bitter attack on Washington, the two former American Revolution partners never corresponded again.

Paine was buried on his farm in New Rochelle. Because his request to be buried in a Quaker cemetery had been turned down and no other cemetery would permit his interment due to his perceived religious apostasy, Paine had arranged for a site on his farm to be set aside for his gravesite. Even so, he expressed a fear that someone might come along and molest his grave. "The farm will be sold, and they will dig up my bones before they be half rotten."[13] A prescient thought, it turned out.

As the story is often told, Madame Bonneville stood at one end of the open grave and directed Benjamin to take a position at the opposite end, "as a witness for a grateful America." As shovels of dirt begin piling up on top of the casket, Benjamin's mother delivered the only eulogy Paine would receive. "Oh! Mr. Paine! My son stands here as testimony of the gratitude of America, and I, for France."[14]

Maybe Benjamin, now thirteen, knew enough to know that America wasn't all that grateful. Maybe he was old enough to understand why. He certainly knew there were only about six attendees at the service, and no one of particular importance. But he knew how important Paine was, having watched, along with others in his family, many notables stopping by to pay him a visit in France and then, later, in America.

Maybe while standing at the open grave, Benjamin let his eyes roam for a moment over the contours of the farm he knew so well, where he and his brother Thomas had spent many pleasant times. He may even have glanced toward the western horizon, thinking of the far reaches of the American frontier that Paine had described. Although he had never actually been west, Paine strongly supported Jefferson's Louisiana Purchase and policies of western expansion.[15] Paine's continental vision, originally expressed in *Common Sense*, 1776, was based on his view that America had unlimited potential, both in territory and uniqueness, ideas that contributed to both American expansionism and exceptionalism.[16] But while standing there, Benjamin surely must have felt some unease about his own future. What happens next? Where do we go from here?

What he probably did not know at the time was that he and his brother would be looked after. Before long they would learn that Paine had left a substantial portion of his estate to Bonneville's mother as a trust for the boys' education. And although very little is known about their early schooling, it is known that in 1813 Benjamin entered the United States Military Academy at West Point at age seventeen. Two years later, he graduated as a brevet second lieutenant in the U.S. Army and began a lifelong career in the military.

As soon as Paine had passed, Madame Bonneville was attacked in the press with allegations of an illicit relationship with him. James Cheetham, a publisher who had been a one-time friend of Paine's but who had become a critic and had quickly published a hostile biography in the year of Paine's death, came to regard him as an infidel. Among other criticisms, he raised questions about the relationship between Paine and Madame Bonneville in his newspaper.

Margaret Bonneville sued for damages. If no well-known people attended Paine's funeral, such as it was, they came out to testify on behalf of Paine in the course of the trial. Among them were inventor Robert Fulton, of steamboat fame; Thomas Addis Emmet, the future attorney general of New York; and J.W. Jarvis, the painter. They knew Paine well and defended his character against Cheetham's baseless accusations. Cheetham admitted in court that he was wrong to allege an improper relationship, saying he had been deceived about Paine by others. Bonneville won her libel suit. But Cheetham got off easy with a small fine. Both he and the judge were religious men; the late Paine, after all, was an infidel in their opinion.

In 1819, Paine's gravesite was robbed and the corpse removed. William Cobbett, an Englishman and publisher in America who was a longtime critic of Paine and his ideas, experienced a change of mind and had Paine's bones dug up. Cobbett took them to England for a proper burial and monument, hoping to honor Paine's memory, since he knew Americans did not. But Cobbett's plans collapsed after no support was shown for his ideas for commemoration, and Paine was never reburied. At Cobbett's death, Paine's bones, which Cobbett had kept, simply disappeared. There was to be no final resting place for the old radical Thomas Paine, though his ideas would live on.[17]

At the time Benjamin became a cadet, his brother Thomas was serving in the U.S. Navy on the second *Wasp*, for which he earned a ceremonial sword for actions in the English Channel during the War of 1812. (The first *Wasp* was captured by the Royal Navy early in the war). But sometime after 1816, all information regarding Thomas and his service in the navy ends. Some authors have said he was lost at sea off the English coast or died on the *Wasp*, but navy records show he served after that ship's return to the United States, and then on another ship, the *Washington*, for almost a year. He resigned from the navy in 1816 and was never heard from again.[18]

There isn't much of a record of Bonneville's time at West Point. A fire at the academy consumed many records. But glimpses of student life there have emerged from time to time. Among these is this one: "Cadet uniforms were blue, with round hat with silk cockade and yellow eagle. Some cadets wore cherry valleys, with buttons along the sides. There were open fires in the rooms and the cadets sawed and split their fuel for their rooms. At the mess there was no tablecloth; the cadets used tin cups and no glasses. The school benches were painted red and the cadets used slates."[19] And there is this description:

In July 1812, there had been a lone cadet at West Point and only one officer, Captain Partridge. Five more students arrived in December. In the spring of 1813, President [James] Madison took an interest in West Point, due to the abilities exhibited by its several score graduates in subordinate positions in the War against Great Britain. Under his urging, cadets of all ages with their warrants, and without benefit of entrance examinations, dribbled into the Academy. Bonneville was one of these. The school buildings were of poor character and it was not until after Bonneville had graduated that a mess hall, academic buildings and two barracks were erected. Living with Thomas Paine in the simple style had probably prepared Bonneville better than most for cadet life. For two years and a half, the young French refugee experienced life under Alden Partridge. The degrading punishment of wearing placards on his back telling of his derelictions, sitting astride a cannon in front of the Superintendent's home for hours for punishment—all these must have been the share of Benjamin Bonneville. Evidently he was not one of Partridge's favorites because some of them were graduated within a year after their entrance; Bonneville stayed longer than most. Since there were no regular examinations, the school year was broken up into furlough periods of odd length, and when in attendance the cadets were followed to petition the Superintendent for even the privilege

West Point, from Philipstown, 1831, aquatint print by William James Bennett. *Library of Congress. Wikimedia Commons.*

of having a part of Sunday to walk about the reservation. There is no record of Bonneville striking up any favorable companionships. Most of his classmates, if they can be called that, with the imperfect system of arrangement, left the Army shortly after graduation. Those who remained found life short and not too sweet, fighting the Indians on the frontiers.... Only a handful lived to see the Civil War.[20]

Benjamin's first assignment following graduation at West Point in 1815 was to a garrison post at Fort Wolcott, Rhode Island. He also served in Massachusetts and Maine and was promoted to second lieutenant. At the end of the War of 1812, Benjamin's father finally traveled to New York, though both boys were away. Irving spoke of Nicholas's bonhomie:

He is represented as a man not much calculated for the sordid struggle of a money-making world, but possessed of a happy temperament, a festivity of imagination, and a simplicity of heart....He was an excellent scholar; well acquainted with Latin and Greek, and fond of the modern classics. His book was his Elysium; once immersed in the pages of Voltaire, Corneille, or Racine, or of his favorite author, Shakespeare, he forgot the world and all its concerns. Often would he be seen in summer weather, seated under one of the trees on the Battery [NY], or on the portico of St. Paul's church in Broadway, his bald head uncovered, his hat lying by his side, his eyes riveted to the page of his book, and his whole soul so engaged, as to lose all consciousness of the passing throng or the passing hour.[21]

Benjamin, Irving suggested, inherited his father's good nature and his "excitable imagination." When Irving first met him, upon the captain's return to the States after his western adventures in 1835, he had this to say: "There was something to the whole appearance of the captain that prepossessed me in his favor. He was middle size, well made and well set.... His countenance was frank, open, and engaging, as well as browned by the sun....He had a pleasant black eye, a high forehead...a bald crown gained him credit for a few more years than he was really entitled to."[22]

In 1819, Nicholas and his wife returned to France. At the end of that year, Benjamin managed to get his first opportunity to head west, by transferring to an army unit sailing down from the East Coast, around Florida to New Orleans. He served in Mississippi supervising military road-building, which included a portion near the well-known Natchez Trace, not far from Jackson. Following that responsibility, he was garrisoned for a time at Bay St. Louis on the Mississippi coast. Then he was promoted to first lieutenant and sent with another unit, the Seventh Infantry, which traveled by steamship up the Mississippi and, for the first time, by steamship up the Arkansas to Fort Smith. He arrived there in 1821.

It was in today's western Arkansas and eastern Oklahoma, what was then part of Indian Territory, where Bonneville got his first taste of America's frontier. He was also stationed briefly in San Antonio, Texas. It was a time of removal and resettlement of native tribes, and the resulting conflicts were not only between the natives and whites—the latter continually pushing west notwithstanding treaty provisions to the contrary—but also among tribes in the area defending (and encroaching upon) their territorial claims. Among the tribes there were Cherokee, Creek, Delaware and Osage. It was also becoming clear that despite their own disputes, the tribes were learning to coordinate pressure on the growing white population. That prompted the United States to establish more forts on the frontier.

Bonneville's responsibilities directly involved Indian affairs. He surveyed lands suitable for tribal placements and helped negotiate various conflicts, both among the tribes and between the tribes and the government. In this

Ball-play (near Fort Gibson, Oklahoma), lithograph by George Catlin. *Library of Congress.*

he proved skillful. Not too long in the future, he would hire several Delaware natives to accompany him on his expedition across the Rockies.

In 1824, Bonneville was transferred to Fort Gibson (Cantonment Gibson) in Oklahoma. The fort was still under construction. And he was promoted to the rank of captain. Soon after, he requested and received a furlough to return to New York and, while there, met up with the Marquis de Lafayette, who was completing a grand tour of the United States. Lafayette had been a major figure in the American Revolution and then later in the French Revolution, until he was captured and held captive by the Austrians during their war with France. A friend of Nicholas Bonneville and of Paine, Lafayette invited Benjamin to accompany him back to France as his aide-de-camp on the frigate *Brandywine*. Bonneville obtained permission from the army and, after arriving in France, ever so graciously requested an extension to his furlough from Major General Jacob Brown, general in chief of the U.S. Army, for twelve months to attend to business in the country:

> *I must ever recollect that it was your friendly exertions alone, that procured me the distinguished honor of being the General's constant companion in his voyage across the Atlantic & of his truly amicable family from Le Havre to*

Paris—also your goodness in requesting me to write to you, if on my arrival at Paris, I found that my business could not be settled within the limits of my present furlough. After this kind interest you have already manifested on my behalf, it is with diffidence I again trespass upon your goodness while I urge the necessity of the continuance of my furlough.[23]

Bonneville's politeness (and flattery) would help him gain leaves of absence and furloughs that his peers in the army sometimes resented. But while in Paris on his extended furlough, he likely visited his mother and aging father, who was by then operating a small secondhand bookstore in Paris. Nicholas died in 1828 in France. Benjamin's mother returned to the United States. She died in St. Louis in 1846.

Following his return to the United States, Bonneville headed back to Fort Gibson. In 1829, he was in Jefferson Barracks, Missouri, near St. Louis, on temporary business for a court-martial hearing. While there, he began to fall under the spell of the writings of Hall J. Kelley and Thomas Hart Benton. Both encouraged exploring the American West. Also, while Bonneville was in Missouri, Andrew Jackson became president of the United States. Jackson one day would play an important role in furthering the captain's military career.

Longing to see the far West after his return to Fort Gibson, in 1831, Bonneville schemed and came up with a plan. He petitioned his commanding officer, Colonel Matthew Arbuckle, for a furlough. He cited family business in New York, and his request was granted.

Back east, Bonneville put his plan into action. He wrote a letter to General Alexander Macomb, commander-in-chief of the army, asking for a leave of absence to lead an expedition to lands west of the Rocky Mountains to determine "the true situation and resources of that portion of our territories." He asked for no expenses and no official command. He would undertake the trip on his own and asked the government only for passports for the expedition. In return for his leave, he would "by observations, establish prominent points of that country, ascertain the general courses etc. of the principal rivers, the location of Indian tribes and their habits, visit the American and British establishments, make myself acquainted with their manner of trade and intercourse with the Indians, finally endeavor to develop every advantage the country affords and by what means they may most readily be opened to the enterprise of our citizens."[24]

Approval was swift. On the one hand, here was a private expedition to the far West that would cost the government nothing. On the other, it was to be organized and led by an officer of the United States Army, and even if unofficial, the government's approval carried clear directives of what it expected the Bonneville mission to accomplish. The captain's leave was approved on July 29, 1831, with the condition that he was to return to his regiment by October 1833. The army expressed interest in what Bonneville was planning to do while on his leave:

> *The leave of absence which you have asked for the purpose of enabling you to carry into execution your designs of exploring the country to the Rocky Mountains, and beyond with a view of ascertaining the nature and character of the various tribes of Indians inhabiting those regions; the trade which might be profitably carried on with them, the quality of the soil, the productions, the minerals, the natural history, the climate, the Geography, and Topography, as well as Geology of the various parts of the Country within the limits of the Territories belonging to the United States, between our frontier, and the Pacific; has been duly considered, and submitted to the War Department, for approval, and has been sanctioned.*[25]

It helped greatly that Bonneville had a schoolmate in New York who had connections with capitalists. Alfred Seton was an associate of John Jacob Astor, the fur trader and financier who established a post at the mouth of the Columbia River, named Astoria, and then lost it after his partners on the West Coast sold out their interests to the British during the War of 1812. With the help of Seton, who had traveled as a young man to Astoria and was saddened to witness the transfer of the post to the British, Bonneville obtained the private funding necessary to outfit and launch the expedition to the far West. Astor likely contributed some of the funds. Seton and Astor still bristled at the thought of losing Astoria. The Oregon Territory was diplomatically unsettled between the United States and Britain since the Treaty of Ghent ended the War of 1812. Bonneville returned to St. Louis, Missouri, in September and spent the winter organizing men and supplies for a large, well-funded fur-trading expedition. By the spring, he was moving his outfit up to Fort Osage.

Although one of Bonneville's documents gives the date of April 30 for the departure of his wagon train, other documents show the date of May 1. By then, everyone was at Fort Osage and ready to go, all 110 men (Irving's number; Bonneville's Report says 121 men) and twenty wagons. It's hard to top Washington Irving's description of the event:

[Bonneville's] *hardy followers partook of his excitement. Most of them had already experienced the wild freedom of savage life, and looked forward to a renewal of past scenes of adventure and exploit. Their very appearance and equipment exhibited a piebald mixture, half civilized and half savage. Many of them looked more like Indians than white men, in their garbs and accoutrements, and their very horses were caparisoned in barbaric style, with fantastic trappings. The outset of a band of adventurers on one of the expeditions is always animated and joyous. The welkin rang with their shouts and yelps, after the manner of the savages; and with boisterous jokes and lighthearted laughter. As they passed the straggling hamlets and solitary cabins that fringe the skirts of the frontier, they would startle their inmates by Indian yells and war-whoops, or regale them with grotesque feats of horsemanship, well suited to their half savage appearance. Most of the abodes were inhabited by men who had themselves been in similar expeditions; they welcomed the travelers, therefore, as brother trappers, treated them with a hunter's hospitality, and cheered them with an honest God speed at parting.*[26]

It's no wonder that readers in the East were fascinated by images such as these. The frontier was the Wild West, and Irving's descriptions, such as the one above, fired their imaginations even more. It's unlikely he lifted these words from Bonneville's journal and expository writing style. Though his journal is lost, the contrast between Bonneville's matter-of-fact writing in his Report and Irving's highly stylized descriptions is clear whenever a comparison can be made of similar events or observations.

But Irving was no stranger to the western frontier, having visited Indian Territory himself. He could tell stories in *The Adventures of Captain Bonneville* from observations or based on the firsthand accounts of others, and he often interlaced Bonneville's observations and descriptions with those of his own while writing his book. But the hoopla and euphoria that Irving depicted about Bonneville's departure from Fort Osage didn't last long:

On the 6ᵗʰ of May the travelers passed the last border habitation. The buoyant and clamorous spirits with which they had commenced their march, gradually subsided as they entered upon its difficulties. They found the prairies saturated with the heavy cold rains, prevalent in certain seasons of the year in this part of the country. The wagon wheels sank deep in the mire, the horses were often to the fetlock, and both steed and rider were completely jaded by the evening of the 12ᵗʰ, when they reached the Kansas

Pigeon's Egg Head (The Light) Going To and Returning from Washington, painting by George Catlin. *Smithsonian American Art Museum. Wikimedia Commons.*

River; a fine stream about three hundred yards wide, entering the Missouri from the south. Though fordable in almost every part at the end of the summer and during the autumn, yet it was necessary to construct a raft for the transportation of the wagons and effects. All this was done in the course of the following day.[27]

Soon after crossing the Kansas, the wagon train entered the first of several Native American villages it would encounter during the course of the expedition. The Kaw (Kansa) tribe was settled around an Indian agency. The tribal chief was White Plume, who had negotiated a treaty with the United States to move to the area as part of U.S. removal policies. In 1821, he had been invited by Indian Superintendent William Clark to visit Washington, D.C., along with a delegation of Indian leaders. The group met with President James Monroe and other officials before traveling to other U.S. cities such as New York and Baltimore.

According to Irving, White Plume and Bonneville struck up an immediate friendship, something that would not be surprising for either man. The captain had a history before his expedition to the Rockies, and after, of establishing friendly relations with Native American tribal leaders. And White Plume, who spoke some English, was known to be welcoming to Whites, at least at that time. He aided the Lewis and Clark expedition several decades before. And it is noteworthy that his great-great-grandson, Charles Curtis, a member of the Kaw tribe, was the first person of Native American ancestry to be elected vice president of the United States, in 1929.

It might also be noted that while Irving wrote often of natives in the vernacular of his times, using words such as *savages* and *squaws*, Bonneville rarely used such descriptions and characterizations in his surviving reports and letters. One story handed down years after his death illustrates the good terms Captain Bonneville had with native tribal leaders, certainly due to his respect for them. At a treaty-making meeting of several tribes in the Fort Vancouver area years after his expedition, Bonneville, who had long ago lost his hair and was called by Native Americans "Chief Baldy" and was now stationed at the fort, asked to attend the meeting, telling the government, "I know these Indians. I speak their language and can be of service to my country, in making a treaty and I would like to show myself to the Indians as a friend." The treaty meeting was held in one of the long buildings purchased from the Hudson's Bay Company at the fort and opened with a potlatch. At the meeting, Bonneville rose and called the chief of the Spokane by name. The chief was surprised but, shaking his head, indicated that he did not recognize Bonneville. Bonneville repeated the gesture for the other tribal chiefs at the meeting, speaking in their languages, but they also did not recognize him. All were polite but felt Bonneville misrepresented his friendship with the tribal leaders. Then, Bonneville sprang to his feet and said, "By the eternal, you shall know me," and pulled off his wig and pulled out his false teeth, and all of the natives immediately recognized him.[28]

Left: Vice President Charles Curtis, great-great-grandson of White Plume. *Wikimedia Commons*.

Right: *Monchousia (White Plume)*, 1822, painting by Charles Bird King. *White House Art Collection, Washington, D.C. Wikimedia Commons.*

These observations and that story aside, it will be shown in this book that Bonneville cannot be held blameless as a leader of his expedition for certain actions that some of his men took against Native Americans.

From the agency near the confluence of the Kansas and Missouri Rivers, Bonneville's expedition continued westward, up the Kansas, up the Republican, to the forks of the South and North Platte. Moving up the latter, he finally reached its branches, crossing the south "Laramie Fork" near the present site of Fort Laramie in Wyoming. Now, one of the most difficult parts of the terrain to get through—hard enough for pack animals and mountaineers, let alone wagons—was just beginning. Quick sands, dry sands, summer heat, little vegetation, rattlesnakes and grizzlies greeted all travelers. In addition, it was Crow country, a tribe that Chittenden described as "polite freebooters."[29] Irving reported that they were "horse-stealers of the first order."[30]

There are stories that back up Irving's claim. One is related to a plains rendezvous:

Horses were always the basic goods of trade. Some, probably the best blooded animals were obtained by legitimate purchase…many more were stolen.…A party of American traders [was] camped with an enormous village—700 lodges—at a plains rendezvous…in November of 1821. Crows were camped two days' journey away, on the Platte, and nearly every night brave young Crows would creep into the very center of this immense camp and steal some of the extra-fine horses that were kept there, under the most stringent security, in log pens.[31]

The Crow called themselves Absaroka (Absahrookee[32])—bird people. And while they mostly abstained from killing White people, stealing from them was another matter. Sometimes, Bonneville still had plenty to learn about natives, especially those perceived to be friendly. Irving told the story of a friendly Crow party meeting up with Bonneville's entourage on June 24 and camping with the group overnight. The band was exceedingly curious about the wagons and especially a cow and a calf among Bonneville's animals. Their conduct, according to Irving, was "friendly in the extreme." But after an evening of pleasantries, storytelling and relaxation, the mountain men woke up the next morning to find the Crows gone, as well as most of their knives and buttons, cut cleanly off their coats. Apparently, the cow and calf were still there, as were all of the horses. This time.

Laramie River, Historic Fort Laramie, Wyoming. *Photo by author.*

Wagon Ruts, Guernsey, Wyoming. *Photo by author.*

Left: *Ho-ra-to-a, a Brave (Crow-Apsaalooke)*, 1832, painting by George Catlin. *Smithsonian American Art Museum. Wikimedia Commons.*

Below: Crowheart Butte, Wind River Reservation, Wyoming. *Photo by author.*

Irving relates another story, this one involving Robert Campbell, a result of an experience he had with a particular Crow chief named Arapooish after some of Campbell's furs were stolen. Campbell had brought some of his furs to the chief's lodge for protection but did not tell him he had others secreted away. Arapooish asked Campbell if he had more furs hidden in a cache. Campbell knew to tell the truth. Crow members had already pilfered the cache, and the chief now told Campbell he knew of the thievery and asked him to determine how many furs were missing. Campbell examined the cache and reported that about 150 beaver skins were missing. The chief promised their return, and within a few days, all of the stolen skins were quietly returned to the cache. As a result, Irving quoted Campbell as saying of the Crows: "Trust to their honor and you are safe; trust to their honesty, and they will steal the hair off your head."[33]

2

"FORT NONSENSE"

Approaching South Pass in Wyoming today from the east is a lovely drive. The gradient ascending the pass is not steep, the road not very winding. The views at pullouts looking to the north and east are expansive. In early summer, when grasses are their greenest and contrast nicely with the red bluffs and highway cuts of Wyoming's Triassic-aged Chugwater Formation, the scenery is splendid. Look carefully to the north and west of the highway, and hints of wagon ruts may still be seen, some merging with more recent vehicle tracks. Those original ruts remind viewers of just how hard and slow it must have been to struggle over rocky terrain and mountains with wagons.

Anticipating the pass summit (7,660 feet) while heading west, modern-day travelers instead find a puzzle. Where's the top? Where's the Continental Divide? One disappointed traveler wrote in 1843, "If you didnet now it was the mountain, you wouldent now it from aney outher place."[34] That undistinguished feature is exactly what Bonneville and his wagons were aiming for. Once there, the party found sandy and sagebrush-covered hills stretching out before them. But first, they had to get there.

Up the lower Republican River, in today's Kansas and Nebraska, the going was pretty smooth, the country "rolling, becoming high level plain as you ascend, the country gradually rising to the West." Then the Platte River, Bonneville's Report stated, "runs through one of the most beautiful and level plains in the world." But arriving at the North Fork of the Platte, things began to change. From the fork of the Laramie River to the Sweetwater, the country was "most horribly broken and difficult to pass.... [T]his county is

Red Canyon, Eastside of South Pass, Wyoming. *Photo by author.*

termed the Black Hills [the country from Laramie fork to the Sweetwater, not the Black Hills of South Dakota and northeastern Wyoming], upon Sweet Water high hills are constantly in view but easily passed, traveling generally on the bank of the river in the sand." But once through it and up the Sweetwater, past Independence Rock (famous today for the signatures of travelers on the Oregon Trail), Devil's Gate and Split Rock, and on toward the Wind River Range, the route became easier.

The Wind River Range peaks, Bonneville noted, were said to be the "highest in the country, about 2500 feet elevated above the plains, and constantly covered with snow." But Bonneville stated that he did not measure them and concluded as to their reputed height, "'tis mere supposition." In our time, the Wind Rivers are known to not be the loftiest peaks in the country, or even in the Rockies. Still, they are rugged and spectacular; early travelers can be forgiven for their misperceptions on seeing them. Irving had much to say about these Wyoming mountains and Bonneville's reaction. It provides a nice contrast to the way the two adventurers penned their descriptions:

> *We can imagine the enthusiasm of the worthy captain, when he beheld the vast and mountainous scene of his adventurous enterprise thus suddenly unveiled before him. We can imagine with what feelings of awe and*

North Platte River, near Casper, Wyoming. *Photo by author.*

Independence Rock, Wyoming. *Photo by author.*

Right: Independence Rock Marker, Wyoming. *Photo by author*.

Below: Devil's Gate, Wyoming. *Photo by author*.

admiration he must have contemplated the Wind River Sierra, or bed of mountains; that great fountain head, from whose springs, and lakes, and melted snows, some of those mighty rivers take their rise, which wander over hundreds of miles of varied country and clime, and find their way to the opposite waves of the Atlantic and the Pacific. The Wind River Mountains are, in fact, among the most remarkable of the whole Rocky chain; and would appear to be among the loftiest....From this great treasury of waters, issue forth limpid streams, which augmenting as they descend, become main tributaries of the Missouri, on the one side, and the Columbia, on the other; and give rise to the Seeds-ke-dee Agie, or Green River, the great Colorado of the West, that empties its current into the Gulf of California. [35]

Indeed, one has to imagine what Bonneville really thought on seeing the Wind River Range for the first time, because, based on his Report, he said very little and said it matter-of-factly. It was a barrier, after all, that he and his men had to find a way across with a wagon train.

But he did note in his Report that the Wind River range is the source of the "Yellow Stone, the Columbia, the Colorado [Green] and the Northern Platte," and by the "winding route" he had taken so far, he estimated that it was about 1,050 miles to get to the head of the Sweetwater (in the Wind Rivers) from his departure point on the Missouri.

Although it is true that near Union Pass in the Wind River Range, west of today's Dubois, Wyoming, is a watershed that divides the waters of the Mississippi, the Columbia and the Green, the latter river in fact empties into the Colorado as it cuts through the parched lands of the desert Southwest and proceeds toward the Gulf of California and is not the source of the impressive Colorado River. Coloradans eventually claimed the source for themselves, noting that the Colorado heads in the northern Colorado Rockies. But Bonneville's observations were noteworthy, nonetheless.

As he traveled through today's Kansas, Nebraska and Wyoming, Bonneville took temperatures and humidity readings and noticed the increasing dryness in the atmosphere. As the party moved west, the woodwork of the wagons started shrinking, affecting the spokes of the wagon wheels, loosening the rims and tires. At length, he took off the iron tire of each wheel, heated it and suddenly cooled it with water, producing a tighter tire to remount on the wheels. As for the men themselves, the increasing elevation and dryness brought on "cramps and colics, sore lips and mouths, and violent headaches." [36]

Where the Clouds Love to Rest, painting by Alfred Jacob Miller. *Dallas Art Museum. Wikimedia Commons.*

Western Kansas, painting by Albert Bierstadt. *Wikimedia Commons.*

As the expedition proceeded southwest toward the head of the Sweetwater, a tributary of the North Platte that empties today into Wyoming's Pathfinder Reservoir, Bonneville took note in his Report of the geology forming the terrain and demonstrated his knowledge of this subject. He noted that the rocks "are the primitive class of Mineral, Granite, Mica, Slate, Hornblende and Lime Rock, without organic relics." He also noted "immense beds of Sand Rock" and observed coal, iron ore, clay, "greasy quartz and Talcose slate." But as it ascended toward the "heads of the Sweet Water," the party encountered immense limestone formations, "filling every mountain and lava filling every plain." One such lava plain, "sixty by forty miles is filled up with large crevices about 15 feet wide and depth unknown, without a drop of water, or the smallest bunch of grass to be found."

But what he didn't know about the geology is that the state of Wyoming had been covered with water. Saltwater. And more than once. Many of the rocks Bonneville observed, especially those thick limestones, were laid down when seawater invaded Wyoming over eons of time. The last invasion, the Cretaceous-aged Western Interior Seaway, divided North America into two land masses around eighty-seven million years ago and continued adding deposition to the seabed and along the shores. The seaway ran from the Arctic Circle all the way to the Gulf of Mexico, almost completely covering Wyoming. Then the land started rising during what geologists call the Laramide Orogeny, seventy to forty million years ago, and the rugged mountains that Bonneville was seeing reshaped the landscape. Of the geology Bonneville was experiencing while heading up the North Platte, Irving had this to say:

> *Every thing around bore traces of some fearful convulsion of nature in times long past. Hitherto the various strata of rock had exhibited a gentle elevation towards the southwest, but here, every thing appeared to have been subverted, and thrown out of place. In many places there were heavy beds of white sandstone resting upon red. Immense strata of rocks jutted up into crags and cliffs; and sometimes formed perpendicular walls and overhanging precipices. An air of sterility prevailed over these savage wastes. The valleys were destitute of herbage, and scantily clothed with a stunted species of wormwood, generally known among traders and trappers by the name of sage.*[37]

Of course, sandstones and limestones were not the only things deposited over millions of years. Near today's Lander, Wyoming, Bonneville found

Sweetwater River, Wyoming. *Photo by author.*

some seeps oozing a thick black substance he had heard about. These "oil springs" had been used for a long time by native people, who "seined off the oil, using the greasy residues for war paint, decoration on hides and teepees, horse and human liniments and other medications."[38]

As to the rivers that the expedition had been traveling along east of the mountains, Bonneville noted that they "increase their size but slowly, [and] upon the banks we find no wood to the North Fork of the Platte, having to cook with buffalo dung, dried weeds." Horses fed on cottonwood, some bitter and some sweet, the latter found in the mountain valleys of "the western waters." In the mountains, he noted, "Pines and Cedars are abundant," as is true today.

It was not the first time that South Pass was used as a gateway through the mountains. But it was the first time someone attempted to take a wagon train across the Continental Divide there. Long before Bonneville, the Shoshone and Arapahoe tribes used the pass while seeking game in the Green River Valley to the west of the divide. In 1812, explorer Robert Stuart, leading a group associated with John Jacob Astor's Pacific Fur Company, "discovered" the pass on an overland trip east from Astoria. Stuart helped establish Astoria after Astor's Pacific Fur Company ship, the *Tonquin*, had rounded Cape Horn and sailed up the Pacific Coast and crossed the bar at the mouth of

Caravan en Route, painting by Alfred Jacob Miller. *Walters Art Museum. Wikimedia Commons.*

the Columbia River in 1811. The ship was blown up when a trade venture with natives near Vancouver Island went awry.

A decade later, Jedediah Smith, one of the great explorers of the American West, noted the pass as a key feature for future travel to the Oregon Territory.[39] By the late 1820s, the pass was being used often by fur traders. In 1830, William Sublette took wagons as far as the Wind River on the east side of the Rockies. He did not, however, attempt to cross South Pass with them. It was the first time anyone took wagons to the rendezvous. And all of them would return to St. Louis following the gathering. But after this trip, Sublette reverted to using pack animals.

Less than two decades after Bonneville's crossing, the route over South Pass was a regular feature of the well-travelled Oregon Trail, with branches on the western side of the divide leading Mormons to Utah and gold seekers to California. But if the pass itself was an easy passage for wagons, the long approach had been another matter entirely. First, there was the terrain. At the forks of the Laramie River near today's historic Fort Laramie, Bonneville found he was "frequently letting my wagons down the bluffs with long ropes 80 men to each wagon," according to his Report. And, according to Irving, Bonneville occasionally had to pull the boxes off the wagons and fabricate a waterproof bottom for them, using tallow and ashes as a tar mixture on hides fixed to the bottoms of the boxes, in order to float them across swollen streams and rivers. Second, this was an increasingly dangerous area of travel due to several hostile (and highly mobile) tribes in the Rocky Mountains, especially the Blackfeet. For decades, they had waged war against the mountaineers and would continue to do so well into the future:

> *Certain Indian tribes were potential sources of hurt: the Arapahoes, Comanches, Utes, Bannocks, and Shoshoni on occasion; the different bands of Blackfeet (Piegans, Bloods, Siksikas) and their neighbors, the Gros Ventres or Atsina, almost invariably. Between 1805 and 1845 the different tribes killed at least 182 trappers, a startling percentage of the relatively small total involved—a thousand or so at the most. There seems no accurate way of estimating how many men were wounded.*[40]

Robert Stuart had turned well south of Union Pass in the Wind River Mountains in 1812, wanting to avoid attacks by the Blackfeet—the "most dangerous banditti of the mountains," as Irving described them.[41] Crossing South Pass instead and reaching the Platte, his route traveled down what became the Oregon Trail, down the Sweetwater and North Platte to the

Wagon Ruts, South Pass, Wyoming. *Photo by author.*

Oregon Trail Marker, South Pass, Wyoming. *Photo by author.*

When Sioux and Blackfeet Met, print by Charles M. Russell. *Library of Congress.*

Platte. Two decades later, as they headed west, Bonneville's party took their wagons up this route to South Pass. But the trail had plenty of challenges for wagons and still exposed his party to roving bands of natives, necessitating a rigorous routine at night to ward off attacks on the wagon train and avoid horse stealing.

Bonneville was trying out a new means of frontier travel. He hoped to save time by not having to unpack and pack the animals each night and morning. Moreover, his method would require fewer horses, he believed, hopefully making his encampments less of a target for tribal raiders. During the day, the wagon train would travel in two columns, with scouts guarding the front, the rear and the flanks of the wagons. At night, the wagons formed a defense, arranged somewhat in a large square with the wagons spread slightly apart, each protected by groups of men. The animals were staked in the center, enclosed by the wagons. Bonneville's party, of course, benefited by including experienced mountain men who had been in the Rockies and who had learned lessons about protection. But it remained to be seen whether his precautions were enough.

The American Fur Company, the company founded by Astor and now headed by Ramsey Crooks, was a dominant player in the fur trade, as had been a large group headed by William Ashley, "Ashley's Hundreds," which eventually became known as the Rocky Mountain Fur Company. (Crooks, it should be noted, was one of the men who had accompanied Robert Stuart in 1812 on his return via South Pass from Astoria.) In 1826, several of Ashley's employees bought him out, among them William Sublette, Jedediah Smith and David William Jackson. Ashley used the profits from the sale to enter politics, and the new partnership lasted until it sold out to new partners, including Sublette's brother Milton and Jim Bridger in 1830. They continued the business as the Rocky Mountain Fur Company. William Sublette, Smith and Jackson shifted their attention to the Santa Fe Trail, where Smith was killed in 1831 on the Cimarron Route by a band of Comanches who happened to encounter him while he was scouting for water. In many ways, the Comanches were just as fierce and feared as the Blackfeet, in their locale of the southern plains, although "the Comanches lived nowhere, but moved with whim and the north wind and the buffalo."[42]

In 1832, Sublette, leading a new expedition, set off for the rendezvous at Pierre's Hole, a spot west of the Tetons set for the annual gathering that year in July. Using a packtrain of 165 mules and horses, he left St. Louis on April 25 and headed up the Missouri, arriving in Independence by May 12. Though he was behind his own schedule, he made it to Pierre's Hole in time for the rendezvous, contesting Bonneville's idea that a wagon train could be a speedier way across the plains. According to Irving, Sublette's party passed Bonneville's wagon train on the way to South Pass, within hailing distance, as it sped by toward the rendezvous.

Bonneville's target, after crossing the pass, also was the rendezvous at Pierre's Hole. He did not make it. On July 20, he spotted the Rocky Mountains for the first time, the Wind River Range. As he continued pushing westward, Bonneville knew he was competing with other companies and free trappers also heading to the rendezvous. Getting there first was a great advantage, because trappers employed by a company could race off to their trapping grounds ahead of the competition, having been resupplied ahead of others. And free trappers could do the same, selling or trading their pelts and picking up new supplies from whomever they could. By now, though, Bonneville knew he wouldn't make the gathering.

Back in St. Louis, another trapping party had decided to join Sublette, as he had the reputation of being "the best guide of the country."[43] Under the leadership of Nathaniel Jarvis Wyeth, a group of explorers made up mostly of recent Harvard and other college graduates decided while heading west that it would be wise to join an experienced outfit. For his part, Sublette was not threatened by this new venture; he knew they were all neophytes and mostly "men of theory, not practice." So, he agreed to lead them into the western landscape and to the rendezvous at Pierre's Hole. They made it, but it was as far west as several members in Wyeth's party got.

The Enlistment, from Eleven Years in the Rocky Mountains, sketch (*Joseph Meek, left, William Sublette, right*). *Wikimedia Commons.*

The rendezvous, held in the summer, was an innovation in the fur trade business. It came about in part with a change in U.S. liquor laws as they applied to American Indians, who hunted beaver, stretched and dried the pelts and took them to trading posts to exchange for goods. Often, they were paid in liquor. Beginning in 1802, U.S. laws were passed regulating trade and intercourse in Indian country. The law generally prohibited traders from selling liquor to Indians. Twenty years later, a new licensing requirement that allowed officials to search for liquor being transported hurt the fixed trading posts but favored the fur traders heading upriver into the plains, partly because of exceptions allowing liquor to be transported by fur-trading parties under certain circumstances. For example, alcohol was permitted to be carried for boatmen moving goods on the rivers.

In spite of all the attempts at regulation during the years of the fur trade, alcohol found its way west to the rendezvous, legally or illegally. In 1832, William Sublette's trading license allowed him to carry a large amount of whiskey for his boatmen. But he went overland to Pierre's

Rendezvous, painting by Alfred Jacob Miller. *Walters Art Museum. Wikimedia Commons.*

Hole that summer without involving any boatmen, thus getting around the regulations.[44] In the same year, a new act of Congress superseded all previous laws and essentially banned all liquor in Indian country. This law stayed on the books for 120 years.[45]

The new rendezvous system also deemphasized fixed trading posts that for years had been established near navigable rivers where furs could be shipped downstream to such depots as St. Louis in the East or Fort Vancouver in the West. With the new model, trappers, many of mixed blood, including French Canadian metis, became independent contractors of sorts, staying year-round in the mountains to trap after being resupplied in exchange for their pelts.

But companies discovered they could also sell goods (traps, brightly colored cloth, buttons, trinkets, scissors and knives, guns and powder and lead to make bullets, etc.) to a much larger gathering of free trappers and natives who gathered on a regularly scheduled basis for the annual event somewhere in the mountains. A larger profit could be made on goods sold at these gatherings, at stiff marked-up prices in the field, than simply obtaining the furs from their own employees and resupplying them for the coming year. And companies still found ways to get around the laws to sell whiskey to natives and everybody else. The rendezvous was an annual event during the fur-trading era, the last being held in 1840 (though a few smaller gatherings continued afterward).

For the mountain men, the occasion was much more than the opportunity for commerce and the chance to resupply for the coming year; it was a highly anticipated social gathering—and a wild party. Picking up letters, newspapers and reports from home from those members of trading companies who had just arrived from the East with their caravans and goods, the trappers reconnected with civilization. Alongside of them, natives set up their teepees, offering their own stock of furs, moccasins, buckskin shirts and their women. As Irving wrote: "Happy was the trapper who could muster up a red blanket, a string of gay beads, or a paper of precious vermilion, with which to win the smiles of a Shoshonie fair one....This, then, is the trappers holiday, when he is all for fun and frolic, and ready for saturnalia among the mountains."[46]

But for the surroundings, it was not a particularly original form of celebration; sailors, cowboys, lumberjacks and prospectors have always tended toward similar entertainments. "The trappers bragged, raced horses, wrestled each other, held shooting matches, gambled, and fornicated. They fought duels and soused themselves and the Indians in alcohol. During their stupors they were gouged unmercifully by the traders, first for cash and then

Cavalcade, painting of rendezvous by Alfred Jacob Miller. *Walters Art Museum. Wikimedia Commons.*

for credit; a man deep in debt was a man whose future catch could, to the extent of his honor, be controlled. Yet to the men themselves and to later commentators, this disregard of money seemed a form of independence."[47]

On July 24, Bonneville and his wagon train left the Sweetwater River and crossed South Pass. They realized as they camped that night that the southward-running stream beside them held trout, a sure sign that they had "turned" the mountains and were now on the western side of the divide separating the waters flowing into the Atlantic or Pacific. The stream was a tributary of the Green River, possibly Little Sandy Creek. In his Report, Bonneville took no note of the fact that he was the first to lead a wagon train over the Continental Divide. But Irving noted that Bonneville now considered himself as having crossed the crest of the Rocky Mountains.

The next morning as the party proceeded toward the Green River, it was overtaken by Lucien Fontenelle's party of the American Fur Trading Company, which had been trailing the wagon train since Missouri but now was rushing on past to get to the Green River. Claiming that Bonneville's train had scattered all of the game and that his party was desperate to get on to the lush valley for the sake of both men and animals, Fontenelle pushed on. It would take Bonneville another day and a half, according to his Report, to reach the river. Then he would move upriver another forty miles before stopping.

Too late for the rendezvous at Pierre's Hole by several weeks now (for both parties), Bonneville decided to settle in not far from the confluence of a stream called Horse Creek and the Green River and build a fort for the winter. But in the course of doing so, he heard that this was not a good idea after all. In time, Fort Bonneville would become known as "Fort Nonsense" and "Bonneville's Folly" among the mountain men for its poor wintertime location and because he abandoned it so quickly after building it.

He apparently experienced no hostilities from a large band of natives found in the Green River Valley at the time. In his Report to Macomb, he had this to say: "[We] fell in with the Gros Ventres of the Prairies, Black Foot, about 900 warriors, had no difficulty with them." What Bonneville did not know was that there had been plenty of "difficulty" with this tribe a few weeks earlier farther northwest at Pierre's Hole. The tribe had fallen back into the Green River Valley after a battle at the rendezvous. But though he was warned about the hostile intent of the tribe by two Crow natives who had recently arrived in the captain's camp, Bonneville disregarded the warning and welcomed a delegation from the Gros Ventres who "saw, no doubt, that everything was conducted [in Bonneville's encampment] with

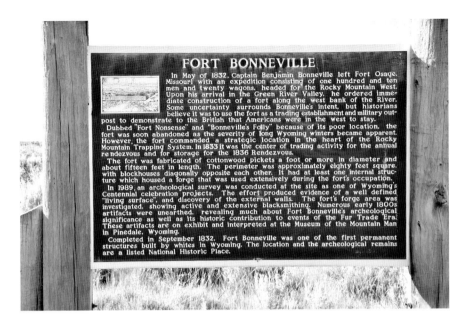

FORT BONNEVILLE

In May of 1832, Captain Benjamin Bonneville left Fort Osage, Missouri with an expedition consisting of one hundred and ten men and twenty wagons, headed for the Rocky Mountain West. Upon his arrival in the Green River Valley, he ordered immediate construction of a fort along the west bank of the River. Some uncertainty surrounds Bonneville's intent, but historians believe it was to use the fort as a trading establishment and military outpost to demonstrate to the British that Americans were in the west to stay.

Dubbed "Fort Nonsense" and "Bonneville's Folly" because of its poor location, the fort was soon abandoned as the severity of long Wyoming winters became apparent. However, the fort commanded a strategic location in the heart of the Rocky Mountain Trapping System. In 1833 it was the center of trading activity for the annual rendezvous and for storage for the 1836 Rendezvous.

The fort was fabricated of cottonwood pickets a foot or more in diameter and about fifteen feet in length. The perimeter was approximately eighty feet square, with blockhouses diagonally opposite each other. It had at least one internal structure which housed a forge that was used extensively during the fort's occupation.

In 1989, an archeological survey was conducted at the site as one of Wyoming's Centennial celebration projects. The effort produced evidence of a well defined "living surface", and discovery of the external walls. The fort's forge area was investigated, showing active and extensive blacksmithing. Numerous early 1800s artifacts were unearthed, revealing much about Fort Bonneville's archeological significance as well as its historic contribution to events of the Fur Trade Era. These artifacts are on exhibit and interpreted at the Museum of the Mountain Man in Pinedale, Wyoming.

Completed in September 1832, Fort Bonneville was one of the first permanent structures built by whites in Wyoming. The location and the archeological remains are a listed National Historic Place.

Road Marker, Fort Bonneville, Wyoming. *Photo by author.*

military skill and vigilance; and that such an enemy was not to be easily surprised, nor to be molested with impunity, and then departed, to report all that they had seen to their comrades."[48] Even so, building a fort may have seemed the smart thing to do at the moment. From Irving:

> *These precautions were, at that time, peculiarly necessary, from the bands of Blackfeet Indians which were roving about the neighborhood....The young braves of the tribe, who are destitute of property, go to war for booty; to gain horses, and acquire the means of setting up a lodge, supporting a family, and entitling themselves to a seat in the public councils. The veteran warriors fight merely for the love of the thing, and the consequence which success gives them among the people....Some of them are armed in the primitive style, with bows and arrows; the greater part have American fusees, made after the fashion of those of the Hudson's Bay Company. These they procure at the trading post of the American Fur Company, on Marias River, where they traffic their peltries for arms, ammunition, clothing, and trinkets. They...have cherished a lurking hostility to the whites, ever since one of their tribe was killed by Mr. [Merriweather] Lewis, the associate of General Clark, in his exploring expedition across the Rocky Mountains.[49]*

In his Report, Bonneville barely mentioned anything about a fort. He only had this to say:

> *Having turned the mountains we struck a large sand plain, upon which we slept without grass or water, having traveled from sunrise till nine o'clock at night.... [N]ext morning started again at daylight and at twelve o'clock had the satisfaction to fall upon the water of the Colorado of the West* [Green River, or various spellings of Seedskedee-agie, meaning "sage grouse"].... [H]*aving ascended this river on the right hand bank forty miles we built a picket work.*

That gave a clue, but not much else. Unfortunately, Irving had little more to say about it as well, describing the fort as a fortified log-and-picket structure. Hiram Chittenden, in his chapter on Bonneville in *The American Fur Trade of the Far West*, added a bit more detail to the fort's description, reporting it as a "typical post" with "palisade walls and flanking bastions at diagonal corners," though where he got his information is unknown.[50]

A detailed contemporary description of the fort and area—one that is very hard to dismiss—was provided by Warren Angus Ferris of the rival American Fur Company, who saw the fort in 1833:

> *Some fifty or sixty lodges of Snakes lay encamped about the fort, and were daily exchanging their skills and robes, for munitions, knives, ornaments, etc., with the whites, who kept a quantity of goods opened for the purpose of trading in one of the block houses, constituting a part of the fort. This establishment was doubtless intended for a permanent trading post, but its projector, who has, however, since changed his mind, and quite abandoned it. From the circumstance of a great deal of labor having been expended in its construction, and the works shortly after their completion deserted, it is frequently called, "Fort Nonsense." It is situated in a fine open plain, on a rising spot of ground, about three hundred yards from Green River on the west side, commanding a view of the plains for several miles up and down that stream. On the opposite side of the fort about two miles distant, there is a fine willowed creek, called "Horse Creek," flowing parallel with Green river, and emptying into it about five miles below the fortification. The river from the fort, in one direction, is terminated by a hold hill rising to the height of several hundred feet on the opposite side of the creek, and extending in a line parallel with it. Again on the east side of the river, an abrupt bank appears rising from the water's edge, and extending several miles above*

and below, till the hills, jutting in on the opposite side of the river; finally conceal it from the sight. The fort presents a square enclosure, surrounded by posts or pickets firmly set in the ground, of a foot or more in diameter, planted close to each other, and about fifteen feet in length. At two of the corners, diagonally opposite to each other, block houses of unhewn logs are so constructed and situated, as to defend the square outside of the pickets, and hinder the approach of an enemy from any quarter. The prairie in the vicinity of the fort is covered with fine grass, and the whole together seems well calculated for the security of both men and horses.[51]

Whatever it looked like, the fort was described as having been sturdily built. Ferris obviously thought the fort was meant to be permanent. But Bonneville's comment that it was a "picket work" does not make it sound that way. Which, of course, raises several important questions, not the least of which is, did a fort actually exist? And, if so, what happened to it?

A recent article questioned the existence of "Fort Nonsense," suggesting it really may be nonsense. Citing all of the accounts and descriptions of Fort Bonneville that the author could discover and based on artifacts from fairly recent archaeological digs at the presumed site that proved indeterminant in terms of their exact origin, he concluded that the evidence is lacking for the existence of anything approaching a fort as Ferris described it. Furthermore, he notes that Ferris is the only contemporary of Bonneville's who offered a detailed description of the fort and is the likely source for the moniker "Fort Nonsense," a name that shows up on a recently discovered map that Ferris had drawn of the area. Perhaps some sort of pen and a shed constructed later on served to corral animals as well as a storage of supplies for the rendezvous that were held nearby for a few years after 1832. Archaeologists have found evidence of a "hard packed floor" area and blacksmithing activity at the site, but it is not certain when those may have occurred or whether they were associated with Fort Bonneville, any subsequent rendezvous or other activities later on.[52]

Still, in spite of a lack of much evidence for the structure, there may have been a U.S. government interest in having some sort of permanent fort built in the area of the Green River Valley. As noted by Bonneville biographer Lovell,

It was poised to cover the South Pass, which led to Salt Lake, Oregon and California. Historian Bernard DeVoto has written, "…the letters of Western traders, the reports of Indian agents, half the press of the United

*States and the speeches of all the Western senators and representatives
were clamoring about the British threat to Oregon. So here was an army
officer trapping furs in the international area, but not many furs. There was
nothing nonsensical in the location of Fort Bonneville."*[53]

In any case, it was abandoned soon after its completion, something
that Chittenden criticized, because Bonneville should have "ascertained"
first that the location was a poor choice before commencing construction.
The Green River Valley may have looked pretty to Ferris, but it welcomed
extreme winter conditions with its sweeping exposure to high winds, blowing
snow and bitter cold. Bonneville was so warned by Joseph Walker.[54] He was
advised to move northwest to near the headwaters of the Salmon River, a
tributary of the Columbia River, in today's Idaho. The route would take him
through Little Jackson Hole (to the south of today's Jackson, Wyoming) and
somewhere over the divide to the west and through Pierre's Hole. Walker
was not the only trapper to warn Bonneville about the poor location on the
Green River chosen for his fort.

But Bonneville had a number of worn-out animals that needed to recover
("recruit" in army jargon) from their journey since the Missouri River, so, he
made arrangements to send some animals and men, under the direction of
a man named A. Mathieu, west to the Bear River with instructions to graze
the animals, and then join him and his party on the Salmon River before the
snow set in for winter.

But what about the wagons? Determining that it was the end of the
road for farther travel northwest with wagons, Bonneville decided to use
a packtrain to move the rest of his party to the Salmon River. And then,
secretly, according to Irving, he had a few of his men at night dig pits and
bury the wagons and a cache of supplies for retrieval the following year
somewhere near the fort. They then covered up the evidence.

This raises a number of questions. First, how to bury a wagon train?
Second, how to secretly get that done? And third, why?

To answer the first question, it is necessary to guess what kind of wagons
Bonneville employed. Unfortunately, there is no direct description of the
type(s) of wagons used. But there are clues. Historians of the Oregon Trail
generally rule out travel with the classic Conestoga-style wagons used in
other parts of America and popularized in Western movies. These large
wagons with their distinctive curved bodies, angled up at both ends, were
simply too big for the Oregon Trail, the box of the wagon measuring
approximately eighteen to twenty feet long by four feet wide. And they

Above: Prairie Schooner, Historic Fort Laramie, Wyoming. *Photo by author*.

Right: Wagon, National Historic Interpretive Trails Center, Casper, Wyoming. *Photo by author*.

were high and deep. The Prairie Schooner was smaller, with its white bonnet resembling a sail in the distance, hence its name, and it was used often on the Oregon Trail. Its body was also four feet wide, but straight and only about ten feet long. At two or three feet deep, the body was lower to the ground. There was another choice available, and that was the freight wagon. These were stoutly built and designed to carry supplies only. And the boxes could be more readily detached, making them easier to float across rivers and streams and, maybe, bury. This seems to be supported by Irving's remark that Bonneville removed the wagon boxes to float them across rivers and streams. Exactly what style of wagons Bonneville used, however, remains unknown.

There is somewhat of a record of the kind of wagons William Sublette employed two years before Bonneville's trip, when Sublette traveled to the Wind River Range, but it doesn't help much. Sublette used ten wagons "capable of carrying heavy merchandise, drawn by mules, and two Dearborn light carriages, each drawn by one mule."[55] Perhaps Bonneville's wagons were similar and were also built in St. Louis by the same companies as were Sublette's. And though Chittenden mentioned the use of oxen as well, Bonneville wrote only about horses and mules in association with his wagon train, at least based on his Report.

In a recent study for the National Park Service about wagons used on the Santa Fe Trail, there are descriptions and some sketches and old photos of wagons of the era and later. But as the author makes clear,

> there is very little useful and reliable information on the wagons that were the backbone of the "commerce of the prairies." This is partly explained by the overwhelming challenge that any researcher faces when dealing with this topic: not one of the countless "prairie schooners" that rolled down the Santa Fe Trail during its long and eventful history is known to have survived into the present day—at least in a complete condition. So, in essence, this is a material culture study in which the material culture is virtually non-existent.[56]

Missourian William Becknell was the first American to take several wagons on the Santa Fe Trail to the Rockies, in 1822. Exactly what kind of wagons he took is not recorded. The same can be said of Bonneville's wagons. But his Report does describe using ropes and eighty men to lower wagons down bluffs, so it may be assumed that his wagons, perhaps loaded, must have been quite heavy. How big and heavy is unknown.

The answer to the second and third questions, about burying wagons in secret, involves a little explanation. Burying caches was common practice among the mountain men, for various purposes. Among others, the men did not want roaming bands of natives to discover them; neither did they want competitors to find them. But Bonneville's effort to hide his caches from many of his own party was based on another common occurrence: losing men to other companies. It was commonplace for men to leave a party in order to join another—or simply leave. In Bonneville's case, he lost some of his Delaware natives when Fontenelle recruited them while on the Green River by offering better terms—$400 per person, which was a large sum. Bonneville quickly learned a new law on the frontier: Loyalty came at the right price.

So, it was necessary to try to keep knowledge of the caches within a close circle of trusted members in hopes the goods would still be there when needed later—and for the right party to find. Exactly how Bonneville managed to keep his numerous wagon caches with supplies hidden is not known. What is known is that his efforts were successful, because he returned to retrieve supplies from such secret places from time to time. It's also known that the buried wagons did not accompany Bonneville back to the States at the end of his adventures in the Rockies.

The idea of burying an entire wagon train has always sounded improbable to many historians. But if he didn't bury them, what happened to them? No real evidence for their remains has ever surfaced, so to speak. Apparently, those wagons, less their goods, remain buried. Forever.

Having chosen to abandon "Fort Nonsense" so quickly, Chittenden stated that the fort was never used again. But evidence suggests that the structure was used again the following year for the rendezvous in 1833 and perhaps later on. But by 1836, when the site was chosen again for the rendezvous, a year after Bonneville had returned to the East, whatever had been built was falling apart. Among the attendees was a missionary, William H. Gray, who wrote that by then nothing was left of the fort but a "square log pen covered with poles."[57] In any case, the site, approximately four miles west of Daniel, Wyoming, on Road 354, was placed in the National Register of Historic Places in 1970.[58] There is a marker describing the fort, and a rock monument dedicated in 1915 has an inscription (barely readable today) that states, "Site of Fort Bonneville, 1832, 1915."

The author has been to the site and has viewed the artifacts collected from the area and given to the Museum of the Mountain Man in Pinedale, Wyoming. It is clear that none of the artifacts on display can be conclusively

Historical Marker, Fort Bonneville, Wyoming. *Photo by author.*

tied to Bonneville, his purported fort or, for that matter, any wagons. The site for the fort is in a pretty setting, all right, but whether there ever was a fort built there or nearby remains a mystery associated with the Bonneville legend.

Still, a structure of some sort must have been erected on or near the site by Bonneville and his men. And that structure likely was a stockade, a term used by a contemporary visitor at the 1833 rendezvous, Charles Larpenteur: "As near as I can remember we reached the rendezvous on Green river on the 8th of July. There were still some of Capt. Bonneville's men in a small stockade. He had come up the Year previous."[59]

This certainly is in line with Bonneville's description in his Report of a "picket work." The aforementioned archaeological surveys did find postholes and several rotted post stumps at the site that seem to support the idea of a stockade-like structure. Although Fort Bonneville, wherever exactly it was located, may have been a poor location for building any kind of permanent structure,[60] the area proved very attractive for summer rendezvous, because six of the next eight such gatherings, beginning in 1833, were held there, including the last one, in 1840. But whether or not Fort Bonneville was more than a well-constructed wood structure meant to serve as the beginning of a permanent fort remains a question open for debate.

One thing is certain: very little trace of a fort, or buried wagons for that matter, has survived. Whether Fort Bonneville was nonsense or not, there is really nothing much to see at the designated historic site today. But the setting is pleasing, and imagination fills in the details.

3

THE MISSED BATTLE OF PIERRE'S HOLE

Preparing to move to the Salmon River for the coming winter, Bonneville packed mules and horses, each with two-hundred-pound loads of supplies according to Irving—two bags on the sides and one on top of each animal. Toward the end of August, his new packtrain left for what is now Idaho. In the Little Jackson Hole area, south of present-day Jackson (upper Hoback Valley), Bonneville reportedly found and buried the bleached remains of two men who had been killed while returning to the States from Pierre's Hole. The attack was by Blackfeet. One of the two men killed was one of Wyeth's men, George More. Curiously, Wyeth also wrote that he came upon the bones of the two men the following year. He also was shown a flask that bore the initials of More by someone who had acquired it while trading with the Blackfeet.[61] The trip out west and Pierre's Hole had not been, it turned out, exactly the kind of adventure some of Wyeth's men had anticipated, including Wyeth's nephew, who decided to return home. Their decision was made before a battle that occurred there as the rendezvous was breaking up.

Pierre's Hole, today's Teton Valley, is a sizeable piece of real estate west of the Tetons. It is named after a chief of the Iroquois who fell there at the hands of the Blackfeet a few years before the Battle of Pierre's Hole. The Iroquois had come to the area to hunt, working their way down from Canada. After the death of their chief, from then on the Iroquois regarded the Blackfeet as mortal enemies.

View of Three Tetons from Pierre's Hole, Idaho. *Photo by author.*

The valley measures approximately twenty to thirty miles long and five to fifteen miles wide, depending on who's measuring, and where. Standing sentinel directly to the east and overlooking the valley are the three distinctive Tetons—at least their upper portions. In fact, it's really when those peaks are viewed from the valley floor directly to the west of the mountains that the French name for the peaks, *Les Trois Tetons*, makes sense: they are the three prominent points that jut up over the tall foothills blocking the view of the rest of the Teton Range.

On one of his trips west, Thomas Moran painted the Tetons from the western side of the mountains. But from Grand Teton National Park on the eastern side of the Continental Divide, it's not so easy to pick out the same three peaks (excepting Grand Teton, which towers above all other peaks in the range from any perspective). From the Jackson Hole side, there are so many more peaks in the range to take in. Indeed, the word for one of the prominent peaks of the Cathedral Group that includes Grand Teton, *Teewinot*, is derived from a Shoshone word meaning "many pinnacles," which is how the tribe described the range. The mountains are more striking from the east, because they rise directly from the valley floor, or "hole," as it was called by the mountaineers. There are few

The Three Tetons, painting by Thomas Moran. *White House Art Collection, Washington, D.C. Wikimedia Commons.*

foothills to obstruct views. Instead, lakes and the Snake River appear at the base of the range on the eastern side, offering a stunning setting.

As John McPhee remarked in *Rising from the Plains*, "Hollywood cannot resist the Tetons. If you have seen Western movies, you have seen the Tetons. They have appeared in the background of countless pictures, and must surely be the most tectonically active mountains on film, drifting about, as they will, from Canada to Mexico, and from Kansas nearly to the coast."[62]

The Tetons are young, geologically speaking, and they are still rising. Yet their core is made up of some of the oldest metamorphic and igneous rocks in North America. And while they indeed rest on a tectonic plate, they are not quite as mobile as Hollywood would have us believe. They are firmly anchored to Wyoming. Thrust up by faults less than ten million years ago and carved by glacial ice, they are among the most jagged peaks in the Rocky Mountains. Oddly, on top of Mount Moran is a remnant of sedimentary rocks the mountain carried all the way up.

Bonneville likely saw the Three Tetons for the first time from the west; the landmarks appear on his map published by Irving in 1837. That was the same year the artist Alfred Jacob Miller visited the rendezvous held in the Green River Valley, along with his patron William Drummond Stewart. Although

The Tetons and the Snake River, photo by Ansel Adams. *Records of the National Park Service. Wikipedia.*

he painted and sketched many scenes of the Wind River Mountains, a search of Miller's paintings does not turn up any definitive depictions of the Tetons. He must not have seen them on his trip out west, for surely he would have painted them.

Today, the Teton Valley in Idaho is rural farming country. In the summer, it is a peaceful setting, as it must have been when the rendezvous was held there. That was not always the case. The 1832 rendezvous was one of the largest gatherings during the fur-trading era, and the most famous. Hundreds of encampments sprang up there in early July, comprising natives and their families, trading companies, free traders and trappers. It was a raucous affair, according to many accounts. Irving described those who gathered there:

> *In this valley was congregated the motley populace connected with the fur trade. Here the two rival companies* [American Fur Company and Rocky Mountain Fur Company] *had their encampments, with their retainers of all kinds: traders, trappers, hunters, and half-breeds, assembled*

from all quarters, awaiting their yearly supplies, and their orders to start off in new directions. Here, also, the savage tribes connected with the trade, the Nez Perces or Chopunnish Indians, the Flatheads, had pitched their lodges beside the streams, and with their squaws, awaited the distribution of goods and finery. There was, moreover, a band of fifteen free trappers, commanded by a gallant leader from Arkansas, named Sinclair, who held their encampment a little apart from the rest. Such was the wild and heterogenous assemblage, amounting to several hundred men, civilized and savage, distributed in tents and lodges in the several camps.[63]

Thomas Fitzpatrick, a partner of William Sublette and Robert Campbell, was a resident "beyond the mountains" at that time and had left Pierre's Hole to meet Sublette and his party on the Sweetwater, to hurry them up. He also wanted to pick up his supplies before the rival companies and traders arrived. He left Sublette, taking two horses with him back to Pierre's Hole—one he rode and one with packs—and he intended to welcome Sublette when he got to the rendezvous. But on his arrival, Sublette discovered that Fitzpatrick had not returned, causing unease. Sublette had cause to be concerned: he and his party had their own brush with Blackfeet in the Wind River country and lost some horses on the way to the rendezvous.

Soon enough, however, Fitzpatrick did appear, emaciated and without his horses but accompanied by two Iroquois who had found him in the mountains. Fitzpatrick had been attacked twice by Gros Ventres in the Green River Valley, losing the packhorse first and then his saddled animal. He had hidden from his attackers with no provisions for a number of days and so was barely recognizable when he made it back to Pierre's Hole.

Toward the end of the festivities, about 150 members of this same tribe were discovered in the area's outskirts. As author Jim Hardee points out, "The Gros Ventres were returning from a long visit with their cousins, the Arapahoe, in what is now the state of Colorado, and heading for their homeland near the Three Forks of the Missouri River."[64] Normally, Hardee notes, the tribe would have returned to their homeland via the Big Horn River, east of the Continental Divide. But they were wary of conflicts with the Crows. He reasons that the tribe, some members of which had attacked Fitzpatrick earlier, was likely trailing him.[65]

Though distinct, the Gross Ventres of the Prairies, as they were then called, were sometimes identified as Blackfeet. Bonneville suggests as much in his Report, seemingly equating the two tribes. Often described as Atsina, the Gros Ventres were closely related to Algonquian tribes, including the

Camp of the Gros Ventres of the Prairies, painting by Carl Bodner, between 1840 and 1850.
Library of Congress. Wikimedia Commons.

Blackfeet.[66] But varying stories of the Battle of Pierre's Hole identify the band involved as either Blackfeet or Gros Ventres. Some members of the Arapahoe tribe, the cousins of the Gros Ventre family, were with the tribe on its journey north to the Upper Missouri, and their oral histories add to the story of what happened at Pierre's Hole. Their histories support the view that it was the Gros Ventres who were involved with the battle. Still, many at Pierre's Hole who wrote about the event later had believed the battle that would take place there involved the Blackfeet.[67]

On July 17, Milton Sublette, Wythe and what remained of his party left the rendezvous, starting to make their way to the Columbia River. But they soon spotted the large band of Gros Ventres. Returning to the rendezvous, they alerted William Sublette and the others, and a party went out to investigate. At the rendezvous were two disgruntled men who had a score to settle with the Blackfeet. Irving told what happened:

> *One of the trappers of Sublette's brigade, a half-breed, named Antoine Godin, now mounted his horse, and rode forth as if to hold a conference. He was the son of an Iroquois hunter, who had been cruelly murdered by the Blackfeet....*

In company with Antoine rode forth a Flathead Indian, whose once powerful tribe had been completely broken down in their wars with the Blackfeet. Both of them, therefore, cherished the most vengeful hostility against these marauders of the mountains. The Blackfeet came to a halt. One of the chiefs advanced singly and unarmed, bringing the pipe of peace. This overture was certainly pacific, but Antoine and the Flathead were predisposed to hostility, and pretended to consider it a treacherous movement. "Is you piece charged?" said Antoine to his red companion. "It is." "Then cock it, and follow me." They met the Blackfoot chief half way, who extended his hand in friendship. Antoine grasped it. "Fire!" cried he. The Flathead levelled his piece, and brought the Blackfoot to the ground. Antoine snatched off his scarlet blanket, which was richly ornamented, and galloped off with it as a trophy to the camp, the bullets of the enemy whistling after him.[68]

William Sublette was chosen to lead a force of mountain men and natives to deal with the threat. In the meantime, the enemy had set up a structure out of branches, a makeshift breastwork—a fort, as the mountain men often called such structures—from which they directed deadly fire as Sublette's group approached. One of Sublette's biographers told the next part of the story:

Sublette, Campbell, a free trapper named Sinclair, and four others crawled up to the edge of the fort. Sinclair, while pulling back a bush to peer at the fort, was shot and had to be sent back to this brother's care. Then another trapper, Mr. Phelps, was hit in the thigh, and a third in the head. An Indian peeped out and was shot by Sublette, but as William reloaded, he in turn was hit in the left arm—the bullet "fracturing the bone, and passing out under the shoulder blade"—and possibly also in the breast. He continued to press the attack, though losing blood, and had to be carried to safety by Campbell, who dressed his wound at a creek and had him taken to camp on a liter.[69]

After a tense night, it was discovered the next morning that the Gros Ventres had slipped away, taking their wounded with them but leaving their dead and many dead horses behind. The battle was over. William Sublette made it back to St. Louis, his arm still in a sling, and eventually recovered. He and Robert Campbell visited with Bonneville at his fort near the Green River on their way east and shared news of the battle, before Bonneville's departure northward to the Salmon River. But Sublette's days as a fur trader operating beyond the Rockies were numbered. He went on with Campbell to establish Fort William near the Laramie River in today's eastern Wyoming

Fort Laramie, painting by Alfred Jacob Miller. *Walters Art Museum. Wikimedia Commons.*

as a trading post. Recognizing that the end of the fur-trading days was coming, Sublette shifted his focus to acquiring buffalo hides. He sold out to the American Fur Company in a few years. The U.S. Army eventually took over the site, renaming it Fort Laramie.

It should be noted that there are many firsthand accounts of the Battle of Pierre's Hole. Fred Gowans's book *Rocky Mountain Rendezvous: A History of the Fur Trade 1825–1840* includes various narratives of the battle by those who were there. A recent study of the rendezvous and battle, based on new material and offering many accounts by participants or observers, is found in Jim Hardee's book *Pierre's Hole! The Fur Trade History of Teton Valley, Idaho.*[70] Many of the firsthand accounts of the battle, as revealed in both books, are contradictory.

Irving's version of the battle in his *Adventures of Captain Bonneville* continues to be retold, even though neither Irving nor Bonneville was a witness. Bonneville heard of the event soon after the battle and obviously recorded details in materials later made available to Irving. But Irving's dramatic storytelling immediately drew criticism from some of the battle's participants, who did not agree with what they read. Many eventually recorded their own recollections. Reading all of these accounts is therefore necessary for a better view of what happened at the Battle of Pierre's Hole.

4

WINTER IN THE ROCKIES
AND A "NATION OF SAINTS"

Before heading north from Fort Bonneville during the late summer of 1832, Bonneville divided his men into four parties, each with a particular mission to accomplish before meeting up again on the Salmon River as winter set in. Exactly when he arrived there is not clear.[71] According to Irving, Bonneville made it to the upper reaches of the Salmon River on September 26 with a small party, having dispersed other parties before leaving the Green River Valley. In his Report to Macomb, Bonneville stated that he arrived at the Salmon on November 10 (a sizeable discrepancy) and awaited the arrival of his hunting parties. His recollection of this date must be an error, for accounts by others of Bonneville's arrival at the Salmon River confirm Irving's date.[72]

According to his Report, Bonneville sent many horses and twenty-one men with a member of his party, identified only as A. Mathieu, a former employee of Etienne Provost, west to the Bear River to recruit them before they were to meet Bonneville at his winter quarters. This group did not show up when expected on the Salmon River, and Bonneville would set out looking for them on Christmas Day.

In addition to that group, Bonneville wrote in his Report that "one of my parties, 21 men among the Crows was entirely lost…and another of my parties on the route through Horse prairie of 28 men lost all their horses, but fighting from 8 a.m. till sun set recovered all but one, taken by the Black Foot and four badly wounded." There was some question for years about who led one of the groups, the party of "21 men among the Crows." Some thought it was a man named (Antonio) Montero, who did join up with Bonneville's enterprise a year later. But recently, it has been shown that this party was headed by David Adams, who was "commissioned in writing to recross the South Pass and trap along the eastern base of the Wind River mountains. He was to go up Shoshone River and the Yellowstone, 'cross over to the Salmon River and descend to the forks [Bonneville's fort].'"[73] That mission did not turn out well, as will be shown later: Adams would be the only one who returned, finally arriving at the following year's rendezvous with tales of desertion and woe.

The other party of twenty-eight men sent up toward the Madison River—or, according to Irving, the Horse Prairie (northeast of the Salmon River cantonment)—fared somewhat better, as the Report indicated, but not without significant troubles with the Blackfeet also. This party was led by Joseph Walker, who temporarily lost a number of horses and mules to native raiders when his guards were relaxing while playing a game of cards. But the mules, upset with the commotion, managed to kick up and throw off their riders, however expert, and soon the raid was abandoned. Walker met up with Bonneville's party at the Salmon River encampment in November, bringing in a few packs of beaver, but the detachment soon left again and was gone over the winter until the next rendezvous, coming up short of trapping expectations on their return to the Green River Valley the next summer.[74]

By the time Bonneville crossed the Continental Divide from Jackson Hole (possibly somewhere south of today's Teton Pass highway) and made it to Pierre's Hole near today's Driggs, Idaho, on his way toward the Salmon River, everyone was gone from the July rendezvous. Irving described the view from the top of the pass: "On the 3d of September he arrived on the summit of a mountain which commanded a full view of the eventful valley of Pierre's Hole, whence he could trace the winding of its streams through green meadows, and forests of willow and cotton-wood and have a prospect, between the distant mountains, of the lava plains of Snake River, dimly spread forth like a sleeping ocean below."[75]

Warren Ferris was also taken with the view from Teton Pass and wrote down an eloquent impression of the scene:

> *Gazing down, in the direction of Jackson's Hole, from our elevated position one of the most beautiful scenes imaginable was presented to our view. It seemed quite filled with large bright clouds, resembling immense banks of snow, piled on each other in massy numbers, of the purest white; wreathing*

their ample folds in various forms and devious convolutions, and mingling in one vast embrace their shadowy substance....Sublime creations! emblems apt for the first glittering imaginings of human life! like them redolent of happiness, and smiling in the fancied tranquil security of repose....Such the reflections suggested by this lovely scene, which, though often on the mountains, I have never before seen below me. Clouds of this pure snow-white appearance, are, however by no means uncommon; but those usually observed beneath us, when on the mountains, have a dark and lowering aspect.[76]

Passing through Pierre's Hole, Bonneville's party observed a less inspiring site: the gruesome evidence of the fight—the bullet-riddled makeshift fortifications the natives had built for defense in a swampy area of trees and corpses the Gros Ventres left behind. But in spite of the battle scene, Bonneville was immediately impressed by the scenery of the Teton Valley, as Irving described it: "The valley of Pierre's Hole is about thirty miles in length and fifteen in width, bounded to the west and south by low and broken ridges, and overlooked to the east by three lofty mountains, called the three Tetons, which domineer as landmarks over a vast extent of country....A fine stream, fed by rivulets and mountain springs, pours through the valley toward the north, dividing it into nearly equal parts. The meadows on its borders are broad and extensive, covered with willow and cotton-wood trees, so closely interlocked and matted together as to be nearly impassable."[77]

Before long, the new winter encampment area was reached. And soon, Bonneville set about building another fort. The Salmon River was aptly named:

The Salmon River is one of the upper branches of the Oregon or Columbia, and takes its rise from various sources, among the group of mountains to the northwest of the Wind River chain. It owes its name to the immense shoals of salmon which ascend it in the months of September and October.... [T]he salmon at their allotted seasons, regulated by sublime and all-seeing Providence, swarm in myriads up the great rivers, and find their way up their main branches, and into the minutest tributary streams; so as to pervade the great arid plains, and to penetrate even among barren mountains....The rapid currents of the rivers which run into the Pacific, render the ascent of them very exhausting to the salmon. When the fish first run up the rivers, they are fat and in fine order. The struggle against impetuous streams and frequent rapids, gradually render them thin and weak, and great numbers are seen floating down the rivers on their backs. As the season advances and the water becomes chilled, they are flung in myriads on the shores, where the wolves and bears assemble to banquet on them. Often they rot in such quantities along the river banks, as to taint the atmosphere. They are commonly from two to three feet long.[78]

Arriving on the upper branches of the Salmon, Bonneville and his party, by now famished and worn out from their push into the region, fell in with a sizeable number of Nez Perce natives, who extended signs of peace and offered Bonneville and his men dried salmon from their own meager supply of food. Bonneville suggested that the Nez Perce—known for their peaceful ways with Whites at that time—camp with him, which they did for a few days. Then, he sent Cerre and a few of his men off with tribal members on a hunting expedition. Cerre was charged with trading with the natives for a winter supply of meat. In the meantime, Bonneville and the remainder of his group moved downstream "five miles below the forks" of the Salmon to establish a winter camp, where, according to his Report, he built two log cabins. This camp, too, he would soon abandon.[79] By all accounts, it was makeshift. Irving called it a cantonment, which seems to be an accurate description. An Idaho milepost near the town of Carmen, Idaho, on U.S. Highway 93 (milepost 310, marker no. 241), carries this inscription, titled "Fort Bonneville":

> *In a grove of cottonwoods across the river, Captain B.L.E. Bonneville established a winter fur trade post, September 26, 1832. His fort— described by a rival trapper as "a miserable establishment"—"consisted of several log cabins, low, badly constructed and admirably situated for besiegers only, who would be sheltered on every side by timber, brush, etc." But several bands of friendly Flathead and Nez Perce Indians camped nearby, and Bonneville fully enjoyed his hunter's life here in the midst of "a wild and bustling scene."*

The earlier quote is from Ferris and appears in Bil Gilbert's book on Joseph Walker.[80] But the last sentence of the highway signpost only hints at what Bonneville and his men really faced during their first winter in the Rockies. The quote is from Bonneville.[81]

There was a lot of activity in the late fall at the Salmon River cantonment. At one time or another, Bonneville was joined by numerous tribes, including Flathead, Nez Perce, Pends Oreille and Iroquois tribal members. Lurking nearby were Blackfeet, a threat requiring constant vigilance. As to

Nez Perce Indians, Montana, photo stereograph, William H. Jackson. *Library of Congress.*

the Flatheads and the Nez Perce camping nearby, Bonneville's Report had this to say:

> *The Flat Heads, 100 warriors with about 150 Nez Percey warriors detatched from the lower Columbia, range upon the heads of Salmon River, the Racine Amere* [Bitter Root] *and towards the three forks of the Missouri. The Flat Heads are said to be the only Indians here, who have never killed a white man, they and the Nez Percey are extremely brave in defence, but never go to war. Are the most honest and religious people I ever saw, observing every festival of the Roman Church, avoiding changing their camp on Sundays tho. in distress for provisions. Polygamy so usual among all indians, is strictly forbidden by them. I do not believe that three nights passes in the whole year without religious meetings. The*[y] *defend themselves from the Black Foot.*

It was clear to Bonneville that rudimentary rituals of the Catholic Church were practiced by several of the tribes encamped near him. These, he was certain, were the result of Catholic missionaries from Canada who had visited the tribes in the past. One story Irving told, based directly on Bonneville's accounts, reveals the strict observance of religious practices among the Nez Perce. He was astonished one morning when four Nez Perce men announced, a few days after refusing to join a group of Bonneville's men departing on the Sabbath to hunt for game, that they were now leaving to hunt, even though among them they possessed just one spear. "What!" exclaimed Bonneville. "Without guns or arrows; and with only one old spear? What do you expect to kill?" The men just grinned among themselves and then bid him adieu. Having first performed some religious rites and seeking the blessings of their wives, "they leaped upon their horses and departed, leaving the whole party of Christian spectators amazed and rebuked by this lesson of faith and dependence on a supreme and benevolent Being." Their faith was rewarded. Soon, the men returned with buffalo meat, which they generously shared with the entire encampment. Pressed by Bonneville as to how they accomplished their feat, the men explained that they chased buffalo at full speed until completely tiring them out and then dispatching them with the spear. Using the same instrument, they then carved up the meat for transport back home. Bonneville expressed nothing but admiration for this tribe: "Simply to call these people religious would convey but a faint idea of the deep hue of their piety and devotion which pervades their whole conduct. Their honesty is immaculate, and their purity of purpose, and their observance of the rites of religion, are most uniform and remarkable. They are, certainly, more like a nation of saints than a horde of savages."[82]

What also became clear to Bonneville as winter approached was that he had too many mouths to feed and depleted forage for his horses and mules, especially with snow on its way. There simply were not enough resources for such large parties of Whites and natives at the cantonment, plus all their animals. Therefore, he once again broke up the men with him and sent some of them off to fend for themselves through the winter months with instructions to meet him the next July at Horse Creek in the Green River Valley. Then, on November 28, he proceeded to the encampments of the Flatheads and Nez Perce, where he intended to await the arrival of his other parties, especially Mathieu's. According to the Report, only Bonneville and about twenty men, plus Cerre and his party, were left at the Salmon River encampment before moving to the Nez Perce camp. Leaving Cerre among that tribe, Bonneville wrote in his Report:

> [O]n the 25 December [Irving says 26] *I started with twelve men in search around the great Shoshone plains in the deep snow, lost one animal frozen to death, reached Lewis* [Snake] *river on the 18 January, here I found one of my men from the Shoshone party,* [Matthieu's party], *finding that not only the mountains were loaded with snow and that my animals were weak, I determined to send for that party to join me immediately, which they did,*

The snow-shoe dance: to thank the great spirit for the first appearance of snow, chromolithograph by George Catlin. *Library of Congress*.

having increased another of my parties in the Shoshone Valley I started on the 19th of February with 18 men to join Mr. Cerre who I had left at the Flat Head town there I again reached on the 14 March.

The story of the winter, as Bonneville indicated in his Report, was one of severe hardship. But it is clear from the start that he had changed plans again and abandoned the idea of wintering near the fort that he had just built. Prior to leaving the cantonment (Bonneville's Report says November 28; Irving, November 20), he once again resorted to burying caches to store goods and materials that would not be needed until later. He sent most of his remaining party ahead of him to the Nez Perce neighborhood so that he could secretly bury his caches. So far as is known, it was a precaution that served him well time and again, as none of his caches were discovered by natives or unauthorized traders during his entire time in the Rockies.

Wanting to procure horses while encamped with the Nez Perce, Flatheads and others in their winter camps, he found little success, as the natives' horses were highly prized. But while he was encamped among them, he began to make plans to strike off to the Snake River plains in search of Mathieu and his party. Before Bonneville left the camp, an illness swept through the natives, probably pneumonia. Bonneville did his best, acting as a physician, to treat the suffering, with some success by employing sweating, bleeding and arranging proper aftercare. He also attempted to convince the Nez Perce and Flathead tribes to try diplomacy with the Blackfeet to reduce tensions. That effort failed, and soon enough, the old enmity between the tribes and the Blackfeet surfaced with a night raid by the latter that gained them a large number of horses the tribes so highly valued but had not taken enough care to protect while in their winter encampments.

Over the next few weeks, Blackfeet raids continued, carrying off more horses. Bonneville had played the diplomat before, but now, in frustration, he advised retribution. Though the chief of the Nez Perce reminded his men of their pacific ways, Bonneville's exhortations riled up some young warriors enough for them to attempt to retrieve the horses. Their effort, however, failed to bring back any except for a few that were too poor for the Blackfeet to bother protecting. But Bonneville, fearing he and his animals might be the next victims of such raids, decided it was time to leave the native encampment. Before he did, he and the tribes moved to a narrow and high valley on a branch of the Salmon River for better protection against the marauding Blackfeet.

According to Irving, Bonneville and his men stayed long enough to witness the wedding of one of their free trappers and a native woman and to celebrate Christmas with a feast hosted by a chief. "After a short prayer, the company all seated themselves crosslegged, in Turkish fashion, to the banquet, which passed off with great hilarity."[83] Then Bonneville and a party of about thirteen or fourteen left to go find Matthieu in the Bear River Valley. Before long, many wished they hadn't left, and a few deserted and headed back to the relative comfort of wintertime tribal encampments.

It was the snow and biting cold of winter, not hostile actions, that almost did in the party remaining with Bonneville. Braving deep drifts, bitter temperatures and near starvation, Bonneville traveled southwest on an unrelenting search of Mathieu's party. One animal froze to death on the journey. At least one of Bonneville's men almost met the same fate. But once Bonneville started out, though admitting he might have thought better of it had he known what he would encounter, he persevered. It was a trait, Irving remarked, that was consistent with everything Bonneville pursued. *Stubbornness* might be a better word.

At some point during the search, Bonneville was struck by the stunning scenery of the rugged country he was traveling through, even in the middle

The Trapper's Bride, watercolor by Alfred Jacob Miller. *Walters Art Museum. Wikimedia Commons.*

of a harsh winter of intense cold and paucity of resources, and he took time to record his impressions. According to Irving, Bonneville penned the following description, showing he could wax poetic on occasion about the western landscape:

Far away…over the vast plains, and up the steep sides of the lofty mountains, the snow lay spread in dazzling whiteness: and whenever the sun emerged in the morning above the giant peaks, or burst forth from among the clouds in his mid-day course, mountain and dell, glazed rock and frosted tree, glowed and sparkled with surpassing lustre. The tall pines seemed sprinkled with a silver dust, and the willows, studded with minute icicles reflecting the prismatic rays, brought to mind the fairy trees conjured by the caliphs' story-teller, to adorn his vale of diamonds.[84]

Making their way down John Day's Creek (today's Little Lost River), the party eventually reached the westernmost of the Three Buttes on the lava plains, plains that spread out like an Arabian desert according to Irving. Fearing their search was about to come up empty-handed, Bonneville's group luckily came upon a native who told them of two men from Mathieu's party near the Snake River. The men were soon found, and they revealed that Mathieu and the rest of his party were on their way to the area. Bonneville was elated. On February 3, 1833, he was reunited on the Snake River with Mathieu, his men and what animals they had managed not to lose while recruiting them. But Bonneville learned that one of Mathieu's men had been badly wounded, and two more men, trying to help the wounded man, were captured by hostiles. Suspecting Bannocks of the attack after seeing among them a horse and saddle from his own party while visiting the tribe, which was encamped close by, he confronted them. The Bannocks blamed the Blackfeet.

Leaving half of his men, sixteen, on the Snake River, under the leadership of a man named Hotchkiss, identified by Irving as Bonneville's clerk, Bonneville and the rest of his men made their way back to the Salmon River caches, which he discovered were secure. Resupplying his free trappers and men, he then prepared for opening the spring hunt and trapping. He sent Cerre and a party out with instructions to meet back on the Salmon on June 15. Then, in the area of the Malad River, Bonneville and his own party set out to trap and find game, only to discover that another group of Whites was heading to the same trapping area. This party was led by Milton Sublette and Joseph Gervais of the Rocky Mountain Fur Company. Because snow impeded both parties' ways, the two groups camped close by for some time, waiting for a thaw sufficient to make a break for the trapping country. On April 25, both groups broke up their encampments. Bonneville and his men reached the Boise River, but trapping success was poor, for both parties as it turned out.

On June 15, Bonneville met up with some of his detachments that had also returned to the Salmon River on time. To celebrate, he distributed plenty of aquavit throughout the camp and gave his men a real "blow out" before making plans to return to Horse Creek the following month for the annual rendezvous. He set out first to look for Hotchkiss and his party left on the Snake River plain. He found him on June 24 near Henry's Fork. Then Wyeth, who was on his way back east and was traveling in company with a group of the Hudson's Bay Company, happened upon Bonneville and his party. The captain, realizing that the goods of that party were a few days behind their leader and Wyeth, thought it might be a good time to jump in and try trading with natives in the vicinity who were waiting to do business with the British company. But after displaying his goods, not a soul "would touch the tempting bait."[85] It was then that Bonneville had his first direct experience confirming the monopoly the Hudson's Bay Company had with tribes in its areas of influence.

During their meeting, Wyeth proposed a joint expedition with Bonneville down the Columbia the following fall for the purpose of reaching Astoria and then heading south all the way to San Francisco. Wyeth was working on a scheme to set up a post on the Willamette River in order to facilitate trade on the West Coast by land and sea. According to Wyeth, Bonneville agreed to his proposal for a joint expedition, but nothing came of their discussions.[86] In the end, Wythe's plans failed. As Irving wrote, "It is needless to go into a detail of the variety of accidents and crosspurposes, which caused the failure of his scheme."[87]

But Wyeth's proposal to Bonneville to go to San Francisco might have proved to be a risky venture. Some writers and historians have stated that it was likely Bonneville would have been restricted from entering certain territories, as he was a military man. Even if Bonneville had undertaken his expedition as a private individual on unofficial business, he may have been under orders not to step foot into any territory below the forty-second parallel.[88] It is curious that in his Report, Bonneville told Macomb that he was planning to go down the Columbia River in the fall and was anxious to visit, among other places, the country "towards the Californias." Perhaps he never intended to go as far as the Mexican Territory. But at the rendezvous of 1833, he would send someone else in his party all the way to the West Coast, well into Mexican Territory—someone with a prearranged passport.

5

RENDEZVOUS AT HORSE CREEK

About six miles west of Pinedale, Wyoming, on U.S. Highway 191, just before an overpass, there is a small marker on the right pointing to a left turn. It leads to Trapper's Point, an overlook of the Green River Rendezvous site. Heading out of Pinedale is a splendid valley with dramatic views of the Wind River Range, also on the right, especially the palisades of Fremont Peak across the valley rising abruptly above the foothills. The flat, grassy valley just east of the highway offered the perfect ground for horseraces that happened here during the times of rendezvous.

After a left turn at the marker for Trapper's Point and then immediately right at another marker, the short drive up a dirt road on a parched, gravely berm ends at a gate. Here, a short walk to the top of the hill reveals an unexpected sight. The contrast between the barren hilltop and the view below to the west could not be greater.

Beneath the hill and spreading out before the viewer lies the verdant course of the Green River. Winding silently, the river makes its way through large cottonwood embankments and lush grasses and willows. The Green is aptly named, especially in summertime. Everything in this valley is some shade of green, an island in a sea of rolling sagebrush plains and cultivated farms. On the distant horizon to the west is the Wyoming Range, still holding pockets of snow in summer. Turn around and look to the east, and one sees the rugged peaks of the Wind Rivers. Hidden from view by the foothills at the base of the mountains is Fremont Lake, the second-largest lake in Wyoming. The Green River Valley is the perfect site for a rendezvous.

Shoshone Indians at a Mountain Lake (Lake Fremont), painting by Alfred Jacob Miller. *Denver Art Museum. Wikimedia Commons.*

And these days, Pinedale carries on the tradition by scheduling an annual weekend rendezvous celebration for citizens and visitors, beginning early in July, just as the original gatherings did.

Six rendezvous were held here during the era of the fur trade, starting in 1833, when Captain Bonneville held the first one in the Green River Valley. The site's stunning view from Trapper's Point was painted by Alfred Jacob Miller when he visited the rendezvous in 1837. A large-scale reproduction of his painting can be seen inside the Museum of the Mountain Man in Pinedale. Back at the top of the hill, interpretative signs describe the panoramic views and what happened here in the past.

If the location of Bonneville's fort—or Fort Nonsense, or Bonneville's Folly, or Bonneyville's Folly, or whatever it might be called at the time and afterward—was indeed a poor site for a fort, it was a superb choice for a rendezvous. Encampments could spread out along the Green River among the tall cottonwoods for shade in the summer in a setting offering plentiful grass for animals and water for all. Historian Robert M. Utley wrote that the

Wind River Range, Fremont Peak in Shadow, Pinedale, Wyoming. *Photo by author.*

"rendezvous of 1833 brought together Bonneville's forces. Some 350 whites and 500 Shoshone, Flathead, and Nez Perce Indians gathered in July on the upper Green, where all could inspect and make fun of Fort Nonsense."[89]

That last comment seems over the top. In fairness, even though Warren Ferris indicated that Fort Bonneville was "frequently called, 'Fort Nonsense,'" it is highly unlikely that those attending the rendezvous in 1833 stood around making fun of Bonneville's fort.[90] Most had plenty of other things on their minds. Besides, there is evidence that the fort's existing structures, built the year before, were still standing and being used as a trading post at the Horse Creek rendezvous.[91]

In any event, attendees in 1833 certainly did not make fun of the place Bonneville chose for a rendezvous; on the contrary, they returned time and again to hold their gatherings there for trading and a good time. As Irving pointed out, whatever conflicts were experienced among the various groups of trappers in the wilderness, they were put aside during the rendezvous:

> *After the eager rivalry and almost hostility displayed by these companies in their late campaigns, it might be expected that, when thus brought in juxtaposition* [at the rendezvous], *they would hold themselves warily and sternly aloof from each other, and, should they happen to come in*

Green River, Daniel, Wyoming. *Photo by author.*

contact, brawl and bloodshed would ensue. No such thing! Never did rival lawyers, after a wrangle at the bar, meet with more social good-humor at a circuit dinner. The hunting season over, all past tricks and maneuvers are forgotten, all feuds and bickerings buried in oblivion.[92]

But there was other business at hand for Bonneville at the rendezvous of 1833. He owed General Macomb of the U.S. Army a report of his progress for his first year in the Rocky Mountains. Though Bonneville had not yet reached the Columbia River, he had already learned much about the far West from many people he met in the Rockies who had been there. His Report would detail, among other things, quite a lot about the strength of the various tribes, information about their location and movements, whether they were peaceful or hostile and other insights about Native American ways. He would also pass along sensitive military observations regarding the numbers and size of British posts along the Columbia River and its watershed. Moreover, Bonneville's Report would make specific recommendations about what the U.S. government should do if it chose to challenge Great Britain and increase its presence in the Oregon Territory.

Bonneville was also trying to figure out how to inform the general that he was planning to overstay his furlough to gain greater firsthand experience before writing more reports and providing additional military information and recommendations. But before finishing his Report, Bonneville first had to hear from his previously dispersed parties and their accounts of what happened while they were away on their winter and spring hunting and trapping expeditions. Their news, he learned, was not very satisfying.

As mentioned in the previous chapter, the party of twenty-one men that Bonneville sent to the region of the Yellowstone was entirely lost except for its leader, David Adams. Bonneville had sent the party for a fall hunt and with instructions to cross over to the Salmon River and meet up with Bonneville that winter. Adams's name is not given in Irving's description of this event in his *Adventures of Captain Bonneville*. Instead, Irving referred to the leader of this group only as "the partisan." (In mountain-man parlance, a partisan is a leader of a detachment from the main party.) Bonneville did not identify the leader in his Report, and it turns out the name was absent in the materials Irving had at hand when writing his account. Hiram Chittenden speculated that it might be Montero.[93]

But Bonneville deliberately left David Adams's name out of his materials, which caused the confusion for years about who "the partisan" was. Adams had signed on to the Bonneville expedition in St. Louis after being paid a generous amount of money, and, curiously, he also signed a commitment "to keep his employer's secrets." After Bonneville had completed his expedition, and in the same year Irving published his work on Bonneville's adventures, Bonneville wrote to Adams inquiring about his welfare and mentioned that Irving's work did not identify Adams's "journey."[94] If Irving knew who the partisan was, he didn't reveal his name. But the partisan's news was not good as Bonneville's Report stated. He and his party had not been seen since the previous year. Irving described what happened. And some of the story was horrific.

Adams and his men fell into a Crow village, and the tribe soon talked most of his men into deserting and carried off horses, traps and other goods of the fur trade. Making his way to a fort on the Yellowstone (later named Fort Cass), he decided to make his winter quarters in the vicinity. But the men who remained with him stole what beaver pelts they could, to exchange for "drunkenness and debauchery." In early spring, he and his men joined up with a few free trappers, and they worked their way to the headwaters of the Powder River. Thinking the area was safe from Blackfeet, in a moment of negligence Adams let his horses loose to graze. Then two warriors from another tribe, the Arikara, entered the camp, feigning friendliness. But Adams wised up to this tactic, and the two were detained by Adams while the rest of the men went looking for their horses. They were too late, they discovered. Indeed, the two Arikara men had been sent into Adams's camp to create a diversion for horse thievery.

Adams became furious and threatened to kill both warriors unless his horses were returned. Realizing that their compatriots were being held, the horse thieves tried to negotiate for their release. But after being offered one or two of the horses in return for the captives' release, Adams refused. He wanted nothing but all of them returned. He threated to burn the two captives alive if his horses were not restored to him. Things quickly fell apart, and as the horse thieves moved away with their prizes, the cries and lamentations of their two brothers left behind could be heard. They tried to escape. Both men were badly wounded and met their fate atop a large pyre of logs that had been set ablaze at the end of negotiations; both burned to death.

It is noteworthy that Irving paused to reflect on the potential consequences of this event: "Such are the savage cruelties that the white men learn to practise, who mingle in savage life; and such are the acts that lead to terrible recrimination on the part of the Indians. Should we hear of any atrocities committed by the Arickaras upon captive white men, let this signal and recent provocation be borne in mind. Individual cases of the kind dwell in the recollections of whole tribes; and it is a point of honor and conscience to revenge them."[95] But though Irving used the word *cruelties*, he passed no moral judgment against Adams or his group, only pointing out how the Whites learned such savage ways and predicting, by way of an explanation, why "terrible recrimination" could be foreseen as a consequence. Bonneville got no blame in the affair. Neither did Adams. But it is clear that the brutal revenge taken on the two Arikara tribal members was directed by Bonneville's partisan. And even though it was a civilian expedition, the captain cannot be held blameless for the actions of his subordinates.

The other party Bonneville sent out the previous year was the party led by Joseph Walker. "Walker also had difficulties over the winter. He had run into strong competition from a group of Rocky Mountain Fur Company trappers under the leadership of Jim Bridger, whose rivalry he had struggled to meet. He had little to show for his efforts."[96]

Still, Bonneville did have some furs to send back to St. Louis in spite of the poor showing for most of his parties. "For the year's catch in beaver, the American Fur Company had 51 packs; the Rocky Mountain Fur Company 62 packs; Campbell, representing the St. Louis Fur Company, 30 packs; and Bonneville, 22½ packs. Bonneville's catch, which represented one year's work and heavy financial output, was very disappointing."[97] It was so disappointing that Bonneville offered $1,000 per man to join up with him for the next year's trapping. But trappers knew that Bonneville's offer was not backed up by any resources other than a fleeting promise riding on the wind. And if trapping and a successful financial return were really Bonneville's objectives, his decision to send Joseph Walker to Spanish California for the following year made little sense.

Publicly, Walker was chosen to recruit and lead a party of about forty men to the Great Salt Lake and spend the year trapping. But everyone knew better, and few would have joined him for that purpose. That, plus the fact that Bonneville equipped Walker's party with a heavy amount of supplies, which would not have been necessary simply to explore and trap around the Great Salt Lake a few hundred miles away, made the argument compelling that the real purpose of Walker's expedition had little to do with exploring and trapping around the lake. Most revealing is the fact that before the Bonneville expedition began, Bonneville had obtained in Washington, D.C., a U.S. passport just for Walker, suggesting that Walker's role with the expedition was meant to be a special assignment from the very beginning.

In any case, the men Walker recruited knew where they were going. Zenas Leonard, Walker's clerk, stated that Walker "was ordered to steer through an unknown country, towards the Pacific."[98] And some of the mountain men who traveled to the rendezvous did so especially for the purpose of joining Walker's expedition, including the Meek brothers, Joseph and Stephen.

All of this contradicts Irving's contention that Walker and his men left the rendezvous for a year's exploration of the Great Salt Lake and then set out on their own for California.[99] And although Irving blamed Walker, who for the second time in two years would show up at the rendezvous the following year with few goods, thereby contributing to the financial failures of Bonneville's expedition, it is clear that trapping was never the real purpose of Walker's participation in the Bonneville venture in the first place.

Over the next year, Walker made what historians regard as the most important discoveries of Bonneville's explorations, because he helped establish the future California and Mormon trails. He reached the Great Salt Lake and went west. Finding the Humboldt River in present-day Nevada, he and his men followed it to the Sierra Nevada Mountains. After Walker repeatedly attempted to cross that barrier, his own stubbornness finally paid off as he found a way through the seemingly impenetrable Sierra Nevada. Some believe he and his group may have been the first White men to overlook the Yosemite Valley as they crossed the mountains. Finding their

Joseph Walker, circa 1860. Photo by Mathew Brady. *Wikimedia Commons.*

way down the ridges to perhaps the Stanislaus River, there is no evidence the party ventured into the valley floor of Yosemite, however.

After crossing the Sierra, Walker made it to the Pacific Coast and then to Monterey. He met with and presented his passport to the governor of the northern Mexican Territory in Monterey, who allowed Walker and his party

Among the Sierra Nevada, painting by Albert Bierstadt. *Smithsonian Art Museum. Wikimedia Commons.*

to winter over in the area. They were permitted to trade while there, just not with the natives. That meant few opportunities for acquiring furs and plenty of time to unload their supplies for little in return. Following their layover and eventually turning to the south and crossing the Sierra at a more southerly location, at today's Walker Pass, Walker and his party headed northeast to the Humboldt River for the return to the 1834 rendezvous.

Coming and going, Walker's party had trouble with natives. Irving identified them as Shoshokoes, or Root Diggers, a derogatory name often used by Whites. They inhabited the deserts and basins of the trans–Rocky Mountain region of today's Nevada and California. According to Leonard, several "disgruntled" members of Walker's party who had lost some of their traps to natives while the party made its way westward toward California took their revenge in early September by killing two of them. It is unclear from Leonard's account if these were the same men suspected of stealing traps. But Irving told the story of one of Walker's men, "a violent and savage character," who vowed "to kill the first Indian he should meet, innocent or guilty" and then killed at least one of two men he found fishing on a riverbank.[100] The Walker men did not tell the captain of their deed (which suggests they knew he would disapprove). Several days later, however, they repeated the act against more natives, and this time they were found out. According to Leonard, Walker "immediately

Half Dome, drawing by Thomas Moran, 1870. *Cooper Hewitt, Smithsonian Design Museum. Wikimedia Commons.*

Monterey, California (Study for Entrance into Monterey), painting by Albert Bierstadt. *Wikimedia Commons.*

took measures for effectual suppression" of these actions, though he did not reveal what those measures were.[101]

But not long after, Walker and his men realized that they were being stalked, perhaps as a result of the killings. Before long, the threat became palpable to Walker, who, after realizing that a very large party of natives in the hundreds was close by, decided this time to take decisive action. Walker sent out some of his men, who immediately surrounded and killed more than thirty warriors who were advancing on the party. This scattered the rest of the band and ended the threat.

Irving told a different version, if it is in fact the same story. Finding a large number of Shoshokoes on the other side of Ogden's River (also called Mary River), which the trappers were about to ford, and believing they were there for hostile purposes, the trappers fired on the group from across the river, killing twenty-five "upon the spot." Irving wrote that it did not "appear from the accounts of the boasted victors, that a weapon had been wielded or a weapon launched by the Indians throughout the affair. We feel perfectly convinced that the poor savages had no hostile intention, but had merely gathered together through motives of curiosity."[102]

These battles have been seen by many historians as overly aggressive reactions by Walker to his and his men's perceived threats from generally peaceful and poor natives. Bonneville also encountered members of this tribe along the Snake River and found them to be "so mild and inoffensive."[103] But there were some outright atrocities committed against more Indians on Walker's return trip from California by several Hispanic horsemen who had joined Walker's party and made a "savage sport" along the way of chasing, lassoing and dragging to death several natives.[104] Bonneville was disgusted at the revelations offered by members of Walker's party on their return and, according to Irving, at the failure of Walker's expedition.

> [Bonneville] *was so deeply grieved by the failure of his plans, and so indignant at the atrocities related to him, that he turned, with disgust and horror, from the narrators. Had he exerted a little of the Lynch law of the wilderness, and hanged those dexterous horsemen in their own lassos, it would but have been a well-merited and salutary act of retributive justice. The failure of this expedition was a blow to his pride, and a still greater blow to his purse. The Great Salt Lake still remained unexplored: at the same time, the means which had been furnished so liberally to fit out this favorite expedition, had all been squandered in Monterey; and the peltries, also, which had been collected on the way.*[105]

But in the end, there is no evidence that Bonneville did anything to admonish Walker. Walker would return several times to California in the 1840s, using his route to lead settlers and then the John C. Frémont military surveying party to Northern California. The latter venture was also likely a disguise, as Frémont, disobeying his military orders not to go farther west than Colorado, went much farther, to California, probably with the knowledge of U.S. authorities. Another guide for the Frémont mission was Kit Carson. A history of their actions in Mexican Territory just prior to the Mexican War makes clear they were there for more than surveying purposes.[106]

The 1833 rendezvous at Horse Creek broke up in late July. Trappers and natives headed off to their fall hunting grounds. Walker and his men left for their less than secretive trip to California. Traveling back to St. Louis with their furs were Robert Campbell, Milton Sublette, Etienne Provost, Michael Cerre, Nathaniel Wyeth (on his way back home from Vancouver on the Columbia) and William Drummond Stewart, a newcomer to the scene from Scotland—of "noble connections," remarked Irving. Bonneville would go as far as the Big Horn Canyon to see his furs and Report off before turning back toward the mountains.

Some $60,000 worth of furs were delivered east that year, either by water or packed down the Oregon Trail. But that was not nearly profitable enough, spread out over all of the fur companies involved. The competition and difficulties obtaining furs were contributing factors to the coming end for the fur-trade era in just a more few years. Edith Lovell argued in her biography of Bonneville that at the 1833 rendezvous he was still solvent. But his expedition certainly was not profitable. Several historians have agreed that Bonneville's 22½ packs of furs barely covered the year's wages for his men, leaving his backers with no return on their investment.[107]

Before the 1833 rendezvous was over, one noteworthy attack—this one not the result of a conflict between natives and Whites—left its mark on this particular gathering. Rabid wolves preyed on some of the attendees, scattered about the rendezvous in their various camps. Attacking in the night, the wolves bit a number of men, and several died soon as a result, or later on. One story Irving relates describes the terror the mad wolves brought into the "folly and frolic" of the rendezvous:

> [A]*n Indian, who was a universal favorite in the lower camp…had been bitten by one of these animals. Being out with a party shortly afterwards, he grew silent and gloomy, and lagged behind the rest as if he wished to leave them. They halted and urged him to move faster, but he entreated them not to approach him, and leaping from his horse, began to roll frantically on the earth, gnashing his teeth and foaming at the mouth. Still he retained his senses, and warned his companions not to come near him, as he should not be able to restrain himself from biting them. They hurried off to obtain relief; but on their return he was nowhere to be found.…Three or four days afterwards, a solitary Indian, believed to be the same, was observed crossing a valley, and pursued; but he darted away into the fastnesses of the mountains, and was seen no more.*[108]

The story (and others like this one) did nothing to help improve the image of big bad wolves. It may have even added credence to tales of werewolves. Certainly, encounters such as this contributed to the demise of wolves over the next century in America. By the late 1920s, for example, the last wolf pack was gone, killed off, from Yellowstone National Park. Curiously, since their reintroduction to the park in the 1990s, no incidents of wolves attacking humans have been recorded. Evidence suggests,

Moonlight, Wolf, painting by Frederic Remington. *Addison Gallery of American Art. Wikimedia Commons.*

however, that wolf attacks on humans, when they rarely do happen, often involve rabid wolves.[109]

On July 25, Bonneville left the Green River rendezvous with fifty-six men and, after crossing South Pass, joined the rest of the eastbound travelers on their way through Crow country and through today's Wind River Canyon to where the Wind River becomes the Big Horn (at the "Wedding of the Waters" near the town of Thermopolis). Because the Arikara were increasingly threatening travelers on the Platte River portion of the Oregon Trail, most of the parties had chosen to go north to float by bullboats down the Big Horn to the Yellowstone and on to the Missouri. Bonneville sent his Report, furs and letters east by way of Cerre, who joined Robert Campbell's outfit carrying furs for the Rocky Mountain Fur Company. Competitors in the field, the companies now helped each other get their goods back to St. Louis.

The trip over South Pass to the Big Horn was not without its "marvels," as Irving called them, or without incidents. As Bonneville and his party made their way down the Popo Agie (Po-PO-zuh) toward the Wind River, he searched for the "great Tar Spring." Finding it a bit east of the Wind River Mountains, he and his men used the oozing black substance as "an ointment for the galled backs of their horses, and as a balsam for their own pains and aches." Irving concluded, from Bonneville's description of it, that evidently the substance was "bituminous oil, called petrolium" and compared it to Seneca oil found in New York.[110] Irving also noted some of the unique features of the country the parties were passing through on their journey to the Big Horn:

> *The Crow country has other natural curiosities, which are held in superstitious awe by the Indians, and considered great marvels by the trappers. Such is the Burning Mountain, on Powder River, abounding with anthracite coal. Here the earth is hot and cracked; in many places emitting smoke and sulphurous vapors, as if covering concealed fires. A volcanic tract of similar character is found on Stinking River, one of the tributaries of the Bighorn, which takes its unhappy name from the odor derived from sulphurous springs and streams. This last mentioned place was first discovered by Colter, a hunter belonging to Lewis and Clarke's exploring party, who came upon it in the course of his lonely wanderings, and gave such an account of its gloomy terrors, its hidden fires, smoking pits, noxious streams, and the all-pervading "smell of brimstone," that it received, and has ever since retained among trappers, the name of "Colter's Hell."*[111]

Colter's Hell is near today's Cody, Wyoming, although the steaming vents John Colter discovered there have mostly become dormant since. Whether or not Colter was the first White man to venture into Yellowstone, it was certainly known to the mountain men who were roaming the country by the 1830s. Even so, many were still not prepared for what they saw. Warren Ferris, accompanied by two natives, went into the Yellowstone area in 1834 and remarked that "the half was not told me" as he encountered the geysers, hot springs, mud pots and steaming terrain of what is now Yellowstone National Park.[112] Little could those who saw Yellowstone then imagine they were traveling within a giant, and active, volcanic caldera, powered by one of the earth's hotspots.

Bonneville's men and Campbell's party reconnected as they proceeded north toward the Big Horn. Campbell related that his men had suffered troubles with hostile natives, this time Shoshones. Having considered the tribe friendly, a small group of Campbell's who were ahead of his main body welcomed several Shoshone men into their camp. During the night,

Geyser, Yellowstone Park, 1881, painting by Albert Bierstadt. *Museum of Fine Arts, Boston. Wikimedia Commons.*

however, the man guarding the horses fell asleep and was shot and badly wounded, with the natives making off with their horses and forcing the men to make it back to the main party on foot.

Big Horn Canyon, on the border of Wyoming and Montana, has its attractions and perils. The trail the trappers used at Bad Pass crawled along the west side of the canyon. Thousand-foot-high Mesozoic and Paleozoic cliffs are prominent in the third-longest canyon in the United States that carves its way through a mostly barren, but colorful landscape. Irving recorded Bonneville's description: "On reaching the…Bighorn Mountains, where the river forced its impetuous way through a precipitous defile, with cascades and rapids, the travelers were obliged to leave its banks, and traverse the mountains by a rugged and frightful route, emphatically called the 'Bad Pass.'"[113]

Exiting the canyon, the Big Horn River lost its rapids, and here the bullboats were constructed to float to the Yellowstone River and down (north) to the Missouri near the Canadian border, passing Fort Cass on the way, an outpost of the American Fur Company. Charles Larpenteur, who was heading downstream in August that year, wrote: "We learned that this

Big Horn Canyon Recreation Area, Wyoming/Montana, photo. *National Park Service.*
Wikimedia Commons.

was a very dangerous post; they had had some men killed by the Blackfeet,
and were even afraid to go out and chop wood. The fort was situated about
two miles below the mouth of the Horn."[114] The company abandoned the
post in 1835.

Arriving at the point on the Big Horn where bullboats were built,
Bonneville—his decision already made to not accompany the parties
downriver to negotiate an extension of his leave—began to execute his
plans to continue through the Rockies and down the Columbia River for
the coming year. It would take a year, until the return of Cerre to the next
rendezvous, to learn whether or not he had the army's blessing to continue
exploring. By then, he felt he would accomplish much more to meet the
army's expectations, and he was confident that his plans for the coming year
would be supported by his superiors. He intended to return to the Wyoming
Rockies and on down the Columbia River after fall trapping.

Bonneville had reservations about Thomas Fitzpatrick, who was making
plans of his own to continue trapping. After helping some of his party
disembark downstream with their furs, Fitzpatrick also returned to the
mountains. So, Bonneville secretly sent out some of his party to a place

Mandan Bull Boat, photo by Edward S. Curtis. *Library of Congress.*

called Medicine Lodge (near today's Hyattville, Wyoming) to get to the trapping areas early. That left him with many extra horses—and only a few men to lead them—to meet up with the rest of his party at Medicine Lodge at the end of August, by the next full moon. But Bonneville managed to reunite with the rest of his men on time.

Once back together, the party worked its way to the Wind River and up the Wind River Valley, trapping along the way. Bonneville was hoping to find a new route through the Wind Rivers over to the Green River Valley, so he engaged in a bit of exploring and mountaineering. Toward the northern end of the Wind River, near today's Dubois, lies Union Pass, a passage then used over the Continental Divide to the western slope of the Wind River Range. But Bonneville didn't take it. Instead, he and a small number of his party moved south toward the Popo Agie, up its tributaries, probing for possible passages through the lofty peaks. They failed to find a suitable route through them to the West. But he and a companion left the main group to see what they could find, and some historians believe the two may have accomplished the first ascent of 13,804-foot Gannett Peak, Wyoming's highest mountain.

Selecting what appeared to be the highest peak around them, they climbed until scrambling on hands and knees, perspiring and peeling off outer layers of clothing. Exhausted, they continued over vast snowfields and up cliffs and false summits on their way to the top. But they persevered and reached it. As Irving remarked, "The pride of man is never more obstinate than when climbing mountains."[115] From the summit, Bonneville "accurately located the faraway Sweetwater, the headwaters of the Wind River, the Yellowstone and the Snake, the Teton peaks, and the fascinating origins of the Green River…which flows north from the western slope of Gannett and over cascades on Wells Creek Fork to Big Bend, where it turns south."[116]

It should be noted that some mountaineers question that the peak Bonneville climbed was Gannett, carefully analyzing his descriptions of streams, lakes and basins and pointing out that all routes up that mountain are moderately technical. Instead, Wind River Peak is more likely the peak he summited. The peak named for Bonneville farther south in the Wind Rivers, which can be seen directly south from Pinedale's main street, is not thought to be a candidate.[117]

After Bonneville and his companion descended from the peaks, the entire party returned to the Green River via the usual route over South Pass, where they picked up supplies at his fort before setting off for Idaho to continue the fall hunt. On Christmas Day 1833, Bonneville and a small party left their encampment for the Columbia River. Over the next two years, Bonneville traveled down the Columbia, twice, though he never reached the Pacific. He noted that he made it far enough to see Mount Hood and "Mt. Baker" (most likely Mount Adams). It is clear from his Report and Irving's account of his journeys that the Columbia was the primary target of his entire enterprise.

But finding that the Hudson's Bay Company continued to refuse to trade with him and help supply his expeditions, forcing him to continue living off the land, Bonneville retreated to the Rocky Mountains ahead of winter each time. There, he had learned how to adapt to the harsh realities of winter and meager supplies, with the help of friendly natives.

After the 1835 rendezvous at the Horse Creek–Green River confluence, Bonneville returned to the States, leaving some of his party in the mountains, including Walker and Montero, to continue trapping. While awaiting a decision on his reinstatement case, and immediately after selling his manuscript materials to Irving, Bonneville organized a small party in the spring of 1836 and made one final expedition to Wyoming, to the Powder River, this time to trade directly with a group of Arapahos. He also tied up loose ends with trappers still connected to his enterprise in the field.

Columbia River, WA, 1909. Wikimedia Commons.

Historical Road Marker near Wind River, Hudson, Wyoming. *Photo by author.*

A story told by Edith Lovell about this last trip is worth repeating. "Captain Bonneville has settled his affairs in this country and is on his way down [to Fort William, now historic Fort Laramie]," reported a trader at the fort. "I'm told he has eight kegs of liquor to dispose of, that we never have too much of, [that] if he will take a reasonable price for I may bargain with him; the Sioux are all along the Riviere Platte and if he should attempt to take it down he's sure to be robbed." As Lovell concluded, it is unknown "whether Bonneville allowed himself to be robbed by the Sioux or by the trader at Fort William."[118]

Ironically, later in his military career, Captain Bonneville finally reached his original destination, perhaps fulfilling the core goal of his expedition to the far West. In 1852, twenty years after first venturing west to Wyoming, he was assigned to command the Columbia Barracks on the Columbia River and served there for three years. The name was changed to Fort Vancouver during his command.

EPILOGUE

The letter Bonneville wrote to General Macomb, the Report as it has been called in this book, was delivered personally by Cerre to the general in Washington, D.C., in 1833. According to a letter written by Cerre in support of Bonneville's appeal to be reinstated in the army, found among the documents in the missing Bonneville army files discovered in the 1920s, General Macomb received the Report (see Cerre's letter of December 9, 1835, to Bonneville reprinted in the appendix). Then it disappeared, not to be found until almost a century later among Bonneville materials that were apparently misfiled by the army.

There is collaborating evidence that Macomb received the Report. A classmate of Bonneville's, Samuel Cooper, an aide at the time to General Macomb, remembered Cerre's letter being delivered to the general. Whether or not Macomb read the Report is less clear. After delivering the Report to the general, Cerre returned that same evening to dine with him, and Macomb's questions to Cerre about Bonneville's future plans strongly suggest the general had not yet read the document. Bonneville made it very clear in his Report what he was planning to do and where he was intending to go for the coming year.

According to Cerre's letter, there was nothing in his encounter with Macomb to suggest that the general was unhappy to learn of Bonneville's plans to overstay his leave. Bonneville's letter did not formally request an extension, and no written reply of approval or disapproval for Bonneville's plans was forthcoming. If Macomb intended to reply formally, he did not get the chance to send it via Cerre. Cerre went on to New York after meeting with Macomb and was supposed to return through Washington, D.C., before heading back to the Rocky Mountains. But due to delays, he did not do so.

After returning from the East and meeting up with Bonneville in 1834, Cerre left the impression that Macomb had no problem with the captain's plans to continue exploring in the far West. But as he indicated in his letter, Cerre also stated that he could not remember for certain whether or not Macomb approved Bonneville's request to overstay his leave. That response probably was not what Bonneville was looking for when he asked Cerre to provide a letter in support of his case for reinstatement. But at the time of Cerre's return to Bonneville's camp in 1834, Bonneville heard what he wanted: there was no reason to believe that his previous year spent beyond the expiration of his leave and continuing plans to explore the West were not supported by his superiors.

Future reports from Bonneville to the army were apparently not received. Cerre was entrusted to mail letters in 1834 in Council Bluffs, Iowa, on his way east later that year, including more reports from Bonneville for the military. The letters and reports presumably were never received and have not been found.

Six months after he hadn't returned to his unit as required by the October 1833 deadline, Bonneville was dropped from the army's rolls. The rumor that he was dead most likely started when he failed to meet one of his parties at the appointed time and place while in the wilderness. Speculation began among some trappers that he must have been killed by natives, and that word got back east. Bonneville learned of this news in his encampment on the Portneuf River before his return.

Back in the States in the late summer of 1835, Bonneville also learned that he had been dropped from the military. It is interesting, as several historians have remarked, that Bonneville made a beeline directly to Astor in New York and not back to his regiment. Perhaps he knew that the latter choice would be futile until he could seek reinstatement. Perhaps he felt a higher obligation to his sponsors. It was in Astor's summer residence at Hell Gate in New York City where Bonneville first met Washington Irving.

As there was a new secretary of war, Bonneville appealed his case to General Lewis Cass (see the September 30, 1835 letter to Cass in the appendix). The army's investigation into Bonneville's request for reinstatement reached all the way to the ears of President Jackson, who made an inquiry asking for verification of Bonneville's claims in his case (see Jackson's request, dated October 1, 1835, in the appendix).

John Jacob Astor, painting by John Wesley Jarvis. *National Portrait Gallery, Washington, D.C.*

After long, agonizing months awaiting word of his appeal while he was residing in Washington, D.C., and working on his manuscript for publication, Bonneville was restored to the military with his former rank following U.S. Senate action in April 1836. (He wouldn't get the news until later in the summer.) This was accomplished even though there had been wrangling over his appeal, not only within the government but also among some rank-and-file officers in his old regiment who had filed a memorial protesting his reinstatement. They clearly objected to Bonneville's special treatment.[119] While awaiting the decision, Bonneville, unable to find a publisher for his saga, approached Irving and sold the manuscript he was preparing for publication to him instead and headed immediately back to Wyoming for his last trip to the Rockies.

It is uncertain if Bonneville's Report to Macomb generated any interest in the army at the time. Whether or not Macomb shared it with anyone before it was lost is not known. Clearly, it was a good thing the Report did not fall into the wrong hands, because its observations on military strength of the British in the Oregon Territory (not great, Bonneville observed) and its open suggestions of just how many U.S. military troops might be required to seize control of British posts along the Columbia River (not very many, he proposed) would have been problematic for the United States. But it is known that some of the items the army acquired from Bonneville upon return from his western journeys, based on records that were not lost, proved useful to the government.

In two U.S. Senate reports in the late 1800s, engineers reported on how good Bonneville's maps were: "The geographic knowledge of the country was greatly augmented in the years 1832–'33–'34 by the examinations and surveys of Captain Bonneville....Captain Bonneville's maps are the first to correctly represent the hydrography of the regions west of the Rocky Mountains, and determine the existence of the great interior basins without outlets to the ocean, to prove the non-existence of the Buenaventura and other hypothetical rivers, and to reduce the Willamette to its proper length." And again:

> *Captain Bonneville's maps, which accompany the edition of Irving's work, published by Carey, Lea & Blanchard in 1837 (the later editions generally do not give the original maps), are the first to correctly represent the hydrography of this region west of the Rocky Mountains. Although the geo-graphic positions are not accurate, yet the existence of the great interior basins (without outlets to the ocean) of Great Salt Lake, of Mary's or Ogden's River (named afterwards Humboldt by Captain Fremont, of the Mud Lakes, and of Sevier River and Lake, was determined by Captain Bonneville's maps, and they proved the non-existence of the Rio Buenaventura and of other hypothetical rivers. They reduced the Wallamuth or Multnomah (Willamette) to its proper length, and fixed approximately its source, and determined the general extent and direction of the Sacramento and San Joaquin Rivers. The map of the sources of the Yellowstone is still the best original one of that region.*[120]

But the evidence for a military purpose in the U.S. Army's support of Bonneville's expedition, found in General Macomb's letter authorizing his leave, and in Bonneville's Report, is highly compelling. Bonneville certainly felt at the end of his first year in the Rockies that he had not yet delivered all of the information the army required of him. There simply had not been enough time. Making it clear in his Report that there was much more to come and that he had not yet made it down the Columbia River or "towards the Californias," he felt that overstaying his leave in order to fulfil his obligations was justified.

Captain Bonneville returned to the U.S. Army at Fort Gibson in September 1836. His commanding officer was not happy with why it took him so long, as he had been reinstated in April. Bonneville soon learned that many of the officers who had signed the memorial objecting to his reappointment were worried about the extra barrier his restored rank presented for their own ambitions for promotion.

After serving in Fort Gibson for several years, he moved with the Seventh Infantry to participate in the Seminole Wars in Florida and then took part in the Mexican War with the Sixth Infantry as Major Bonneville, where he was wounded during the Battle of Churubusco. He was subject to a court-martial after that action, due to one of his disgruntled officers having seen his brother shot and killed in front of him, though several officers testified to the major's courage during the battle and that the two brothers were not anywhere near each other on the field. But even though the major was found "not guilty" on most of the counts against him, it was determined that he was "guilty" of three. The final outcome admonished him for a lack of "due exertion and activity," per general orders, but nothing more. Nevertheless, the verdict was hard on Bonneville.[121]

He went on to serve in numerous other places, including Nebraska, Lake Ontario, Vancouver Barracks and New Mexico, and he served as a recruiting officer in St. Louis and then as a commanding officer of Benton Barracks, St. Louis, during the Civil War. His first wife and daughter died there in 1862.

In 1865, Bonneville was promoted to brevet brigadier general, a reward for his long years and service in the U.S. Army. He commanded Jefferson Barracks in St. Louis until retiring from the army in 1866.

In 1871, Bonneville married Susan Neis, many years his junior at age twenty-five. They lived in St. Louis and then in Fort Smith, Arkansas. Some thought it was a marriage in the "European style" (to pass along his estate), but other accounts describe a happy marriage.[122] He died in Fort Smith on June 12, 1878 and is buried at Bellefontaine Cemetery in St. Louis. At the time of his death, he was the U.S. Army's oldest retired officer.

Most historians and other writers give Benjamin Bonneville a failing grade as a fur trader and explorer. There is little question, however, that by leading a wagon train across South Pass in Wyoming for the very first time, he helped pave the way for future travel on the Oregon Trail and its Utah and California pathways and contributed directly to American expansionism.

While it is not known for certain just how much Bonneville's expedition of 1832–35 and the materials he brought back with him, many of which were lost, informed national priorities and decisions about the American West, what is clear is that Captain Bonneville found a way, with official blessings, to have the adventure of a lifetime. After noting his accomplishments and long service in the military, an army obituary described Bonneville as living a "quiet, happy life" when he

American Progress, print, after 1872 painting of the same title by John Gast. *Library of Congress*.

passed away.[123] But his own contentment may have been less certain, for Bonneville soon missed his time spent in the western wilderness. Having returned to civilization after his sojourn to Wyoming and beyond, he found a moment to reminisce, as Irving quoted him:

> *Though the prospect of once more tasting the blessings of peaceful society, and passing days and nights under the calm guardianship of the laws, was not without its attractions; yet to those of us whose whole lives had been spent in the stirring excitement and perpetual watchfulness of adventures in the wilderness, the change was far from promising an increase of that contentment and inward satisfaction most conducive to happiness. He who, like myself, has roved almost from boyhood among the children of the forest, and over the unfurrowed plains and rugged heights of the western wastes, will not be startled to learn, that notwithstanding all the fascinations of the world on this civilized side of the mountains, I would fain make my bow to the splendors and gayeties of the metropolis, and plunge again amidst the hardships and perils of the wilderness.*[124]

Appendix

THE LOST 1833 REPORT
AND RELATED DOCUMENTS

AUTHOR'S NOTE: The following report and letters come from several sources, but mostly from the *Annals of Wyoming* (vol. 8, no. 4, April 1932). Except for the letter to Macomb (The Lost Report), no edits have been made beyond those found in the original printed sources. The Macomb Report has been lightly edited by the author for two reasons. One, a few of the annotations needed updating based on new information that has become available since the original annotations were published. Annotations are in brackets in the document. Two, previous transcribed versions of the Report do not always concur. The author used a copy of the microfilmed original handwritten Letter to Macomb, available in the Bonneville folder (no. 448) at the Oregon Historical Society Research Library in Portland, Oregon, along with available published transcriptions, to determine the necessity for making a few new edits. Bonneville's original spelling, punctuation and grammar are retained as much as possible.

***

Letter from Captain Bonneville to Major General Macomb (The Lost Report)

Crow Country
Wind River
July 29, 1833

General
This country I find is much more extensive than I could have expected, as yet, I may say I have actually visited, only, the heart of the Rocky Mountains, or

in other words the head waters of the Yellow Stone, the Platte, the Colorado of the West [Green River], and the Columbia. I have therefore remained, I hope I have not trespassed too much upon your goodness, to explore the North of the Columbia in the Cottonais [Kootenai] country, and New Caledonia [British Columbia], to winter on the Lower Columbia, and going to the South West toward California on my return, which will certainly be in the course of next fall. I would not have presumed this much, were I not aware how desirous you are of collecting certain information respecting this country, and my return at present would have afforded but half a story, which would have been laughable in the extreme. I have constantly kept a journal, making daily observations of courses, country, Indians, etc., in fine, of every thing I supposed could be interesting. The information I have already obtained authorizes me to say this much; That, if our Government ever intend taking possession of Oregon the sooner it shall be done, the better, and at present I deem a subalterns command equal to enforce all the views of our Government, although a subalterns command is equal to the task, yet I would recommend a full company, which by bringing provisions to last till June could then live upon the salmon, which abounds there [on the Lower Columbia] during the summer and fall, and farming for themselves for the next near could subsist themselves well, five men there would be as safe as an hundred either from the indians [Chinookan] who are extremely peaceable & honest, or from the establishments of the Hudson Bay Compy. who are themselves to [too] much exposed by their numerous small posts ever to offer the least violence to the smallest force. They have a trading post at the Mouth [Fort George, Astoria] of three or four men to oppose all trading vessels, another above, <u>Vancouver</u>, which is strongly built, and capable of a garrison of one hundred & eighty men, here they have farms, mills etc. & every convenience of old settlements, manned by half breeds, indians and some Canadians, but they are generally distributed in trapping companies who frequently remain about a year. Walla Walla [Wallula, Washington] a post still higher up, on the left bank of Columbia, handsomely built, but garrisoned by only 3 to 5 men, may easily be reduced by fire or want of wood which they obtained from the drift. Colville [Kettle Falls, Washington] another post upon the North Fork, is also feeble, 3 to 5 men there to keep up a connection and trade. The Returns from Vancouver, Walla Walla & Colville, do not exceed 3000 skins, which may be considered trifling for their expense, but from New Caledonia to the North of Columbia, and from towards the Californias their returns are immense; these are the countries I have not yet examined and am now so anxious to visit.

As to the cultivation of the bottoms of the Columbia, the lands are of the best, the timber abundant, but it is deluged at the rise of the river, but the

Multnomah or as it is named here the Wallamet [Willamette], runs through one of the most beautiful, fertile and extensive vallies in the world, wheat corn and tobacco country.

The Hudson Bay at present have every advantage over the Americans. Woolens at half price flour and tobacco they raise, horses they obtain from their indians at 1$ prime cost, shells they fish for, and their other articles of trade reaching them by water in the greatest abundance and at trifling expense, compared to the land carriage of the Americans, that the latter have to avoid their rencontre by every means in their power, not only on the Columbia, but also even on the Colorado [Green River], the Head waters of the Arkansas, the Platte, the Missouri; they even speak of making a Fort on the Big Horn to oppose the American Fur Company. So you see, the Americans, have, to as it were to steal their own furs, making secret rendezvous and trading by stealth.

The History of the Country is this, first the Hudson Bay entered it in 1810 trapping & trading generally employing between 80 & 100 men, gradually increasing their present number of about 280 men. The A. M. Compy [American Fur Company] about 1816 sent Imel and Jones with about 30 men, who remained about 5 years then totally defeated by the Blackfoot indians on the Yellow Stone. Mr. Henry also entered it about the same time of Imel & Jones with about 80 men, built forts on the Big Horn on Lewis [Snake] River and on the three forks of the Missouri was also defeated by the Black foot indians on three forks. In 1825 Genl. Ashley came in with about 50 men met the Hudson Bay on Lewis [Snake] River. On the point of Fighting with them, however took from them the Iroquois and their furs, subsequently himself was defeated by the Arrapahoes [Arapahoe] on the Head Waters of the Colorado, and lost all his horses, 120 head. Ashley then sold out to his clerks Smith, Jackson and Sublette who raised their number to 130 men, who in 1830 themselves sold out to their clerks & best trappers, Fitzpatrick, Younger Sublette, Bridges, Frap & Jarvie who now remain in the country with about 80 to 90 men. Drips, Fontenelle, Pilcher, Vanderburgh & Benjamin came in a firm in 1827 with about 75 men, reached the Head of the Platte there lost all their horses by the Arrapahoes there caching the greater part of their merchandise and packing their men in the winter got lost in the deep snow finally dispersed Drips, Fontenelle & Vanderburgh offering their services to the A. F. C. [American Fur Company] increased their number to 160 men. Gantt came up in 1831 with about 50 men, mostly afoot done [did] little then retired to the head waters of the Arkansas where I understand he has opened a trade with the Camanche, the Arrapahoes, and Shians [Cheyenne].

The above I think will give you a tolerably correct idea of the great quantities of Furs [that] must have been taken from the country in order to keep alive so many companies at such great expenses in men and horses. This country may be said at present to be poor, but beaver increases so rapidly that any part permitted to rest three years is said to be as rich as at first the companies therefore endeavor to ascertain each others hunting grounds and to conceal theirs and even their successes or disasters. Last year Fitzpatrick's company in their 2 years trapping sent down about 150 packs, 60 skins per pack; A. M. C. last year one years work sent about 31 packs. This year A. M. C. & Fitzpatricks appear to have each about 44 packs, and sustained great loss in horses taken by the Aurickeries [Arikara]; again the same party lost 17 men by desertion taking each 2 horses and six traps.

As to the Indians, that the Pawnees [Pawnee] reside on the lower Platte in several bands, amounting to about 1200 warriors, they are well mounted, and war with the Crows [Crow]. The Sioux, Shians and Arricories, make their hunting grounds in the Black Hills, 2500 Sioux, 400 Shians, 160 Arricories, they reside on the Missouri and wage war upon the Crows, and Pawnees. They are extremely warlike and are well mounted. The Crow Indian range upon the Yellow Stone and head waters of the Platte, about 1500 strong in three villages fight with the Black Foot, and the Arrepohoes. The Crows have good horses and I believe the best buffaloe country in the world. The Arrepehoes range upon the heads of the Arkansas and Canadian [rivers] and are very numerous, fight also with the Shoshones.

The Shoshones a poor unwarlike race, some few who have arms and horses venture to descend into the plains in villages, but they are generally dispersed by twos and threes into the mountains without horses, without arms but the stone pointed arrow, and depending upon their numerous dogs to take the Mountain Sheep, they are met with in almost every mountain running from every body, and are termed Digne de Pitie i. e. Worthy of Pity, they will steal and kill whenever a good opportunity offers, their villages are generally more friendly tho dangerous to be met alone. They range about the Salt Lake.

The Bannocks in villages about 400 warriors mostly afoot live about the falls of Lewis [Snake] River, there during the salmon months catching and drying salmon, and in the fall move up that river to the Great Plain, and hunt the buffaloe which they dry and return to their falls, unwarlike defend themselves from the Black Foot. The Flat Heads 100 warriors with about 150 Nez Percey warriors detatched from the lower Columbia, range upon the heads of Salmon River, the Racine Amere [Bitter Root], and towards the three forks of the Missouri. The Flat Heads are said to be the only Indians here, who have never killed a white man. They and the Nez Percey are extremely brave in defence, but never go to war, are the most honest and religious people I ever saw, observing every festival of the Roman Church, avoiding changing their camp on Sundays tho, in distress for provisions.

Polygamy so usual among all indians, is strictly forbidded by them. I do not believe that three nights passes in the whole year without religious meetings. The[y] defend themselves from the Black Foot.

Descending the Columbia waters. The great body of the Nez Percey and the large bands of the Pends Oreilles. Here horses may be said to abound, some individuals having from 2 to 3,000 head, upon which they live, together with roots. The Cootenais [Kootenay] 200 warriors, having the other day commenced a war with the Black Foot have been driven from their original grounds upon the Northern Branches of the Columbia and have joined the Flatheads. The numerous herds of Indians upon the head waters of the Missouri and its Northern branches are in one term the Black Foot Indians, the Blood, the Sarcies, the Piedgans, and the Gros Ventres of the Prairies are those most troublesome in these mountains. The[y] are well mounted abundantly supplied by the richness of their country in excellent shotguns and ammunition. They are extremely numerous. When the snow begins to fall bands from 3 to 400 men move with their families all afoot and packing dogs, locate themselves some bands in the Shoshone country, some toward the Nez Percey etc. build stone forts then despatch their most active men to steal horses and to kill their nearest tribe, and as the snow melts in the spring gradually retreat with their spoils to their own country. When the grass is found sufficient, bands of about the same size leave their families and move to the plains in all directions to kill and steal. The only security against these Indians is to fight from the bushes in the plains 'tis most certain destruction. The whites are unsafe with any tribe except the Nez Percey and Flat-heads, true parties of size are unmolested, save by the Black Foot but individuals must be careful of the Bannacks, the Shoshones, the Arrepehoes, the Shians, the Pawnees, the Crows.

As to the Whites, they have their leader, a trader, his hired men, also what is termed free men, men who join or runaway from other companies and going to the next, remain with it in the following manner; if they have horses & traps of their own, they agree to sell all the furs caught at $4 per lb. purchasing all their supplies from that company, if they have no horses and do not wish to hire, they are then loaned horses & traps and are to sell their beaver unskinned at 4 to $5 each paying for their supplies and loss of traps. And the great object of companies is to catch these men on the way to their rendezvous and trade all their credits, with whiskey, tobacco etc. In the winter the parts of the same company meet & pass the winter together, separating in the spring & again meeting at some other place for their summer rendezvous, where the supplies from St. Louis are expected each company, generally, having a place of its own. Rendezvous are certainly the scenes of the most extreme debauchery and dissipation.

Prices at the Ms. [Mountains]

Furs—vary from.. $3 to 5 per lb.
Skin Trapping do [doz.] .... $ 4 to 5 per ps. [piece]
Blankets colored... 18 to 20 ea.
Tobacco... 2 to 3 per lb.
Alcohol... 32 per gallon
Coffee.. 2   " tin cup, a pint
Sugar.. 2   " do
Flour... 1   " do
Shot guns, prime cost—4$... 40 ea.
Rifles   "   10$... 60 do
Horses.   20 to 25$..................................... 120 to 250 ea.

The customary price as a year's wages from 250 to 400$. As to the prices and regulations of the Hudson Bay I know but little, but this summer, fall and spring I believe I shall be able to explain all their regulations of trade etc.

On the 30th of April I left Independence with 121 men and 20 wagons. On the 12 May crossed the Kansas, kept up the left bank, move up the Republican which I headed, having at first gone through a rolling country upon the republican I marched upon an elevated place, then struck it a little west and in one day fell on the Platte, the 2nd of June, here found the river 3/4 mile wide. The banks 2 to 3 feet high river about 4 feet deep but full of quicksands; the plains upon the banks of the Platte are from 3 to 5 miles wide and I marched to the forks 130 miles without a break or creek. At the forks I first found buffaloe 45 days from the settlements. Having gone up the south fork about 10 miles I crossed this fork, the river below I measured 1 3/4 mile wide in two places, general width 1 1/4 mile, cut the tongue of land and fell upon the north fork. Here the river plain is small bluffs of immense size putting in to the river, finally reached the main Branches of the north fork, crossed this south, *Laramies Fork*, there began one of the most broken countries I ever beheld, frequently frequently letting my wagons down the bluffs with long ropes 80 men to each wagon at last we came to the main forks of the north forks, having cut the tongue of land to the north and in two days came to Sweet Water, which we ascended on the right bank to Wind River Mountains, having turned the mountains we struck a large sand plain, upon which we slept without grass or water, having traveled from sunrise till nine o'clock at night, next morning started again at day light and at twelve o'clock had the satisfaction to fall upon the water of the Colorado of the West [Green River] having ascended this river on the right bank forty miles we built a picket work.

Fell in with the Gross Ventres of the Prairies, Black Foot about 900 warriors, had no difficulty with them. Here we remained to recruit our horses then went a North West course and on the 10th November fell upon Salmon River where I again built two Log Cabins and waited for my men.

One of my parties, 21 men among the Crows [David Adams] was entirely lost, another of my parties of 21 men [A. Matthieu] by the Shoshones lost 7 horses and 4 men, and another of my parties on the route through Horse prairie [northeast of Salmon River encampment], of 28 men [Joseph Walker] lost all their horses, but fighting from 8 a. m. till sun set recovered all but one, taken by the Black Foot and four badly wounded.

On the 28 November, some of my parties had returned. I then proceeded to the Flat Heads and Nez Perceys, where I intended to wait the arrival of the remainder of my parties. At last on the 25 December I started with twelve men in search around the great Shoshone plains in the deep snow, lost one animal frozen to death, reached Lewis [Snake] river on the 18 January. Here I found one of my men from the Shoshone party, finding that not only the mountains were loaded with snow and that my animals were weak, I determined to send for that party to join me immediately, which they did, having increased [?] another of my parties in the Shoshone Valley I started on the 19th of February with 18 men to join Mr. Cerre who I had left at the Flat Head town, there I again reached on the 14 March, and on the 18th proceeded with 23 engages and 14 indians, Nez Percey and Flat Heads toward the Comanche [Camas] Prairies laying on the route to the Lower Columbia. On the 6 April came to the mountain [north of Blaine County, Idaho] which I found impassable and remained at its base till the 27 May at which time I succeeded in passing losing 4 horses and two mules then continued to the West fell Bosy [blurred], Malade, Comanche, Boisey and La Payette Rivers. At last I found that living upon fish, horses and roots would not do, I then tried to cross the mountain to the North 1st July [June], the great depth of snow forced me to seek another pass, at last reached the Forks of Salmon River on the 15th of July [June], here I waited 4 days for my parties, having found their path I took it and on the 29th found them, [Hodgkiss], Much to my surprise with the Pends Orreilles and the Cottonais (Kootenai), the Flat Heads and Nez Percey having been driven from the country by the Black Foot, who that spring consolidated for that purpose, here I remained with these people till the 5th July. The Black Foot being at that time quite near, made me fear to cross the prairies with my small party of 23 men. I therefore induced these friendly indians by presents, to march upon the Black Foot towns and pretend to war, while I pushed across the plains, and on the 23rd reached the valley of the Colorado, [Green River], here I found so many buffaloe carcasses and these only skinned that I actually feared to approach the Rendezvous and at night sent two men to examine it, had the satisfaction to hear all was well I then continued and next day met all the whites in the country, and on the 25 [July] started with Mr. Cerre to escort him to the Big Horn, which I expect will take me till the 10 Augt. I will then proceed to the North West towards the North of the Columbia.

The country upon the Lower Republican [Kansas and Nebraska] is rolling, becoming high level plain as you ascend, the country gradually rising to the West, the Platte runs through one of the most beautiful and level plains in the world, upon the North Fork the country becomes much broken, from Laramies Fork to Sweet Water is most horribly broken and difficult to pass, this county is termed the Black Hills, upon Sweet Water high hills are constantly in view but easily passed, traveling generally on the bank of the river in the sand; The Sweet Water heads into the Wind River Mountains, said to be the highest in the country, about 2500 feet elevated above the plains, and constantly covered with snow. I have not measured these mountains, 'tis mere supposition. In the same bed of mountains rises the Yellow Stone, the Columbia, the Colorado and the Northern Platte. They are extensive and exceedingly difficult to be gone through, and are always turned. The General course I traveled to head Sweet Water was about West North West, and estimated by me at 1050 [miles] by the windings of the route. From the Forks of Horse Creek of the Colorado [Green] to the head of Salmon River (Idaho) the route lays generally through a country easily passed, with the exception of two mountains which must be gone over. One is low, the other must be passed upon the river, and upon a cornice of the mountain from which horses fell from every party, descent perpendicular 270 feet high [Near Snake River]. Course to the Salmon N. West. 350 miles. Here again begins a bed of mountains lying North and South from the extreme North to a great distance to the south, about the big Salt Lake, these again form the Southern bank to no person knows where, however this much is known, that every river even all creeks run through Cannions or Columnar blocks of Limestone, Greenstone trap. To the North a little east lays immense plains; to the South a little east are the great Shoshone plains. To the South a little west lyes immense plains of sand, without water, without grass. To the West is a rough broken country and West of North is the Cottonais Country, remarkable from the great quantity of wood, and its difficulty of passage. The Black Hills are the primitive class of Mineral, Granite, Mica, Slate, Hornblende and Lime Rock, without organic relics. Yet occasionally I would observe immense beds of red Sand Rock. Some places saw Slate, Coal, Iron Ore, in one place only I found small quantities of greasy quartz and Talcose slate.

As we ascended the Sand Rock and Clay prevailed, which yielded upon the heads of Sweet Water, when began an immense region of Lime Rock, filling every mountain, and Lava every plain. In one of which sixty by forty miles is filled up with large crevices about 15 feet wide and depth unknown, without a drop of water, or the smallest bunch of grass to be found. The Rivers to the east of the mountains increase their size but slowly, upon the banks we find no wood to the North Fork of the Platte, having to cook with buffalo dung, dried weeds, occasionally however we find the yellow or bitter cotton wood. Above this and through the Black Hills we have the Sweet Cotton wood, upon which we feed our horses in the winter, and become extremely fat. Above this and upon the western waters the bitter cotton wood prevails; upon the mountains the Pines and Cedars are abundant.

The thermometer with me ranged at sunrise through the summer at about 47° at 2 p. m. 72°. Once I saw it as high as 91°. During the winter months, in the vallies where we wintered it stood generally about at 12 p. m. 26°. I left it and traveled across the plains, where the cold was much more severe. I find that at 25° my feelings were much as they would be in the states at 13° but the heat of 72° as oppressive as that of the states of 100°. Soil of the Platte and other Rivers from the east are intirely unfit for cultivation, these of the west are much the same till we reach the Boisy a branch of Lewis River, the soils here are excellent but not extensive. The Buffaloe range from North to South, beginning about the Forks of the Platte, and extending to a line running from about the Forks of Salmon River to the east of the Big Salt or Eutah Lake, then running so as to strike a little North of Tous [Taos]. West & south of this line not a buffaloe can be seen; elk, deer, sheep, and bear can be had for a small party to subsist excepting some large sand plains where nothing' can be found. The Big Salt Lake I have never seen, but I am told it has never been traveled around; five trappers once attempted to coast it, and were near dying from hunger & thirst.

Thus much, General, I have been able to collect in compliance with my promises, and I hope will be satisfactory when you consider, how extensive this country is. An individual in the states goes his 40 to 50 miles easily but here, when we have to feed our horses on grass and being closely tied up every night, requires time to feed morning, noon & night, makes our Traveling very slow. I omitted to state that the horses here are generally about 14 to 14 1/2 hands high, stout built, and upon which the Indian will gallop all day. The mode of traveling here, is this. The Indians in villages at 8 a. m. raise camp, the chief leads upon a fast walking horse, the whole, men, women and children follow, the women with their lodges, poles and baggage, while the men ride totally unencumbered, at 10 or 11 a. m. the chief pitches his lodge, the camp is then formed extending along the river or creek, making for each lodge a small brush pen to secure their horses from their enemies; besides planting an 18 inch stake into the ground with a cord attached to the horses fore foot. In the morning the horses are turned out at clear day light, making their camps or journeys about 8 miles long. The whites travel much in the same way, making however longer journeys.

In the course of a few days I shall be on my route to the Cottonais country, and round by the lower Columbia to the South. On my return about the last of June [1834], I shall meet Mr. M. S. Cerre and if you shall have any instructions for me, shall be glad to receive them, either to join any party that might be sent, to comply with any other commands in this country, or to return to the States.

I have the honor, to be, General, with every consideration Your most obdt. svt. [servant]
B.L.E. Bonneville Captain 7 Infy

***

Recd. 26 Sept.
Washington City
Sept. 26, 1835
To the Honorable Lewis Cass
The Secretary of War.

Sir,

I have the honor to report my return to this city, from a long and perilous tour of exploration beyond the Rocky Mountains, upon which tour I have used every exertion to collect information relative to that country and the tribes of Indians that inhabit it, together with maps and charts.

I set out upon my tour with the consent of the War Department, and was charged by General Eaton, then Secretary of War, with instructions to guide me in collecting information with which he considered it advantageous for the government to be possessed, during my absence and at a time when a report of my death by the Indians received general credence my name was stricken from the rolls of the Army.

The object of this communication, is, to request, that my name be restored.

I have the honor to be Very respectfully
Your Obdt. Svt.
B.L.E. Bonneville

***

St. Louis 9th Dec. 1835.
Dear Sir

In 1833 I was charged by you with a letter addressed to Gen. McComb, which I have delivered myself to him; the letter was not read in my presence, but on returning to Gen. Mc. that same evening he then told me that your letter had given him great satisfaction. He asked me several questions relative to your expedition; such as has Capt. Bonneville taken any observations on his rout, does he keep a minute of his travels, did he go into Oregon, where was he to go when you left at the Big Horn, when will he return to the U. States, &c. In answering the latter, I told him that it was impossible for you to return in due time to comply with your furlough; but you expected to be permitted to remain in the mountains a longer space of time so as to be able to give a general satisfaction—I stated to you in July, 1834, at the Little Lake that it was more than probable that Gen. McComb should have written to you had I returned through Washington, & that a longer absence should have been granted you.

It may be that Gen. McComb told that your furlough should be continued for a longer time; but I cannot say positively that he did. However I confess that it was my impression at that time, as well as at present, the Government was satisfied that you should remain some time in the mountains for the sake of acquiring information.

The above statement is to the best of my knowledge. Nothing more for the present, but remain your
Most Obedient Servt &
friend,
M.S. Cerre.

***

Washington City,
September 30, 1835
To the Honorable Lewis Cass,
Secretary of War.

(Excerpt)

Sir:
In obedience to your orders I have the honor to report, that in August 1831, I received a furlough from the Commanding General of the Army, to expire in October 1833, with a view of proceeding to the mouth of the Columbia River, and exploring the' tract of country between the settlements of the

United States and the ultimate point of destination—I hereby have to remark that the: lateness of the season, when my furlough was granted, absolutely precluded my leaving the settlements until 1st May 1832—thus in the very onset nine months of my furlough were consumed. The plan of operations presented to the Commanding General was submitted to the Department of War, and approved & with my furlough received instructions to collect all the information in my power, touching the relative positions of the various tribes of Indians in my route, their numbers, manners and customs, together with a general history of the country through which I was destined to pass. On the 1st May 1832 I departed from the Frontiers of Missouri with a number of men I had hired for that purpose—My route lay up the Kansas, the Main Platte, its northern branches and Sweet Water, and reached the waters of the Colorado of the West, in the latter part of August, 1832. Finding that this long journey had very much weakened my horses and that my men were yet badly qualified to feed themselves in small game, when they could scarcely do it among the buffaloe, I determined to travel north into the lands of the Nez Perces, Flat Heads, Cottonais and Pend' Oreilles, where I would find game for my men, and plenty of grass and bark for my horses and at the same time to become particularly acquainted with these several tribes. As soon as the snow had disappeared in the spring 1833 I proceeded to the Big Horn River, by the south point of Wind River Mountains and continued down that river to where it became navigable. Here I halted, made boats & having engaged a Mr. Cerre with several men to proceed to the States and gave him a report for the Commanding General, stating that the shortness of my leave of absence made it impossible for me to accomplish the objects contemplated at starting, within its limits, therefore requested its extension—at the same time reporting the progress I had made. This report cannot now be found in the Office of the Adjutant General; but Captain Cooper recollects such an one was received. As the application for an extension was made several months anterior to the expiration of the furlough already obtained—having scarcely commenced collecting the information desired and believing there would not be the least difficulty in obtaining a further extension of furlough, I determined to prosecute the object originally intended and proceeded down the Big Horn which runs nearly north giving the advantage of latitude so high, that I could easily cross over the heads of the Yellow Stone, to the northern branches of the Columbia, and winter near the Sea—and that in the Spring I could return upon its Southern branches—which plan I attempted to execute; but finding so much hostility on the part of the Black Foot, that it was impossible to advance without continued fighting and severe loss in men and horses. As several battles had already been fought with these Northern tribes, I found it absolutely necessary for me to retreat by the south point of the Wind River Mountains, by doing which I reached the Bannock's late in the winter, 1833, and my men passed the remainder of that season with them. Constantly intent upon getting to the lower Columbia, I left my party with the Bannocks tribe and on the 25 December 1833 started with three men down Snake river in order to ascer-tain the best manner of entering the vast wilderness still to the west, leaving instructions with the party in my rear to descend Snake River the moment the winter broke up and meet me in my ascent. In obedience to these instructions the party started, but finding that I did not arrive at the point proposed, after tarrying until they had exhausted every means of subsistence, they determined to abandon the route, and returned above the Bannock tribe, to the buffaloe ground, where I overtook them on the 16th June 1834—once when I learned they had relinquished the prosecution of their route under the belief that my party of three men and self had been killed & they had so reported. Knowing that Buffaloe were generally plenty upon the heads of Black-Foot and Portneuf Rivers I determined to go there and make meat sufficient to subsist my party on its descending the Columbia. Upon this route I fell in with Mr. Cerre 28th June 1834, the gentleman to whom I had eleven months before entrusted my communications to the General in Chief, which he informed me, he had delivered, and that the general appeared perfectly satisfied with my Report and also with my determination to persevere in the course I had adopted, and pursued, that owing to his remaining longer in New York, than he had originally contemplated, he was prevented returning to Washington and consequently had left the former city without bringing an extension of my furlough or any communication whatever from the Dept. of War. Highly gratified at the verbal report of Mr. Cerre of the flattering expressions made by the General in Chief, I was inspired with renovated ardor for the enterprise I had undertaken being now determined to accomplish it at all hazards. Previous to putting this intention into practice I had prevailed upon Mr. Cerre to take charge of my letters and reports to the General in Chief, General Eustis and other gentlemen, which although he had now become attached to the American Fur Company and felt some delicacy in doing, he did promise to forward them to their various addresses, upon his reaching Council Bluffs. These letters owing to causes impossible for me to explain, I regret to state, never reached their destination, which appears to have been the fate of most of the communications made to the States & which it was next to an impossibility to accomplish without employing persons expressly for that purpose....

Believing now that I had fully executed the order of the General in chief and that from my maps, charts and diary I would be able to furnish the Department of War, with every information desired, respecting the Rocky

Mountains and the Oregon Territory I therefore congratulated myself with the pleasing anticipation that in the spring I should be able to leave this cold and solitary region for the more genial one of society and civilization. Accordingly, so soon as the snows had melted away I moved eastwardly to the Popo Agie river, where I lay to give my horses flesh and good hoofs for the long rout of returning home, which I did by the head of Powder River and its mountains, arriving at Independence Missouri the 22d August 1835. Imagine then, upon my return to the settlements, what must have been my mortification, when instead of the approbation I expected for my exertions and enterprise, I learned my name had been dropped from the rolls of the Army and the consequent loss of my commission which I held dearer than life.

Raised at the Military Academy, I became as it were identified with the Army; 'twas my soul, my existence, my only happiness and at a time, that I was exerting every nerve to win the approbation of my superiors—I find myself branded as a culprit—'tis mortifying indeed—My character as a soldier has been fair too long—to believe my superiors will hesitate one moment to restore me my character and my rank.

I have the honor to be, Sir, Very respectfully,
Your most obdt. svt.
B.L.E. Bonneville
Late Capt. 7 Regt. U.S.Infy.

***

Capt Bonneville to Sec of War
Endorsed by President [Jackson]
B.25 W.D. [War Department] copied
Filed with 2742 A.C.P. '78
1 October 1835
Com'ing General
Report Recd 19 Nov

Returned to the Department for a report whether the communication alleged to be made by Capt Bonneville was received at the Department and whether the Commanding Genl. Approved of his Capt Bonneville continuing his exploring expedition, and gave the messenger to understand that his furlough would be extended.
A.J. [Andrew Jackson]
Referred to the Major Gen for a report of the circumstances on his return.
L.?. [Either L.C. or L.L.]
5 Oct '3

NOTES

Introduction

1. Bagley, *South Pass*, 67–68; Josephy, *American Heritage Book of Indians*, 350.
2. Irving, *Three Western Narratives*.
3. Abel-Henderson, "General B.L.E. Bonneville Letters," 220.
4. Ibid., 207. It is worth noting that a researcher said to have found the Report in the Bonneville army files, Dr. Howard Hamblin, also claimed to have found the missing journal among other materials. But a footnote (page 608n) identifying all of the material found in the army files does not include any mention of a journal.
5. Chittenden, *American Fur Trade of the Far West*, 305. Chittenden, it should be noted, engineered the first road built in Yellowstone National Park.
6. Irving, *Astoria*.

Chapter 1

7. Irving, *Three Western Narratives*, 645.
8. Lovell, *Benjamin Bonneville*, 11.
9. There is conflicting information about the year of Bonneville's birth. His tombstone in the Bellefontaine Cemetery in St. Louis reads 1793. The few records that survived a fire at West Point many years ago, including

those of Bonneville, also indicate a birth date of 1793. Many authors, however, accept the birthdate of 1796.

10. Clark, *Thomas Paine*, 322.

11. Paine, *Complete Writings of Thomas Paine*, 2:921. The author of this book sees no reason to doubt Paine's story.

12. Ibid., 2:1467.

13. Nelson, *Thomas Paine*, 325.

14. Quoted in Hawke, *Paine*, 400.

15. Conner, "Presidential Power."

16. Conner, *Thomas Paine*, 34. Also, see Restad, *American Exceptionalism*, 45.

17. Conner, *John Adams vs. Thomas Paine*, 96–97.

18. Lovell, *Benjamin Bonneville*, 20–23.

19. Neilson, "Captain Bonneville," 209.

20. Baumer, *Not All Warriors*, 10–11.

21. Irving, *Three Western Narratives*, 629.

22. Quoted in Lovell, *Benjamin Bonneville*, 90.

23. A copy of Bonneville's letter to Major General Jacob Brown reporting on his travel with Lafayette to France and requesting an extended leave may be found in the Bonneville folder no. 448, Oregon Historical Society, Portland State Library, Portland, Oregon, https://ohs.org/research-and-library.

24. Lovell, *Benjamin Bonneville*, 50.

25. Irving, *Three Western Narratives*, 995–96.

26. Ibid., 645–46.

27. Ibid., 646.

28. Mrs. James B. Montgomery, a talk on "Captain Benjamin," Oregon Historical Society, Bonneville folder.

29. Chittenden, *American Fur Trade of the Far West*, 308.

30. Irving, *Three Western Narratives*, 656.

31. Josephy, *American Heritage Book of Indians*, 379.

32. Field, *Prairie and Mountain Sketches*, 66.

33. Irving, 772–73.

Chapter 2

34. Bagley, *South Pass*, 290.

35. Irving, *Three Western Narratives*, 664–65.

36. Baumer, *Not All Warriors*, 21.

37. Irving, *Three Western Narratives*, 661.
38. Roberts, "Oil Business in Wyoming."
39. Oregon Encyclopedia, "Jedediah Strong Smith."
40. Lavender, *Rockies*, 92. For another look at the mortality rates of trappers in the West, see Hannon, "'A Life Wild and Perilous'," 58–77.
41. Irving, *Three Western Naratives*, 669.
42. Graves, *Goodbye to a River*, 20.
43. Sunder, *Bill Sublette*, 103.
44. Chittenden, *American Fur Trade of the Far West*, 35.
45. Martin, "'The Greatest Evil'," 2432.
46. Irving, *Three Western Narratives*, 761–62.
47. Lavender, *Rockies*, 90.
48. Irving, *Three Western Narratives*, 684.
49. Ibid., 669–70.
50. Chittenden, *American Fur Trade of the Far West*, 308.
51. Gowans, *Rocky Mountain Rendezvous*, 774–80.
52. Eddins, "Was Fort Bonneville Really Nonsense?," 20–33.
53. Lovell, *Benjamin Bonneville*, 68. The quote from DeVoto, *Across the Wide Missouri*, 58–59.
54. Gilbert, *Westering Man*, 111.
55. Sunder, *Bill Sublette, Mountain Man*, 84–85.
56. Gardner, "Wagons on the Santa Fe Trail," v.
57. Lovell, *Benjamin Bonneville*, 101. Also see Eddins, "Was Fort Bonneville Really Nonsense?," 25–26.
58. Barnhart, "National Register of Historic Places Inventory—Nomination Form: Fort Bonneville."
59. Gowans, *Rocky Mountain Rendezvous*, 813–15.
60. After visiting the site, the author's wife observed that this location would be a terrible choice during any kind of flooding of the Green River; the site, just yards away from the Green River, would be quickly inundated. And floods certainly have occurred on the Green near Daniel, Wyoming, where a gauge nearby exists to monitor water levels. See Carter and Green, "Floods in Wyoming."

Chapter 3

61. Hardee, *Pierre's Hole!*, 293.
62. McPhee, *Rising from the Plains*, 128.

63. Irving, *Three Western Narratives*, 675.

64. Hardee, *Pierre's Hole!*, 249.

65. Ibid.

66. Josephy, *American Heritage Book of Indians*, 262.

67. Ibid., 186–262.

68. Irving, *Three Western Narratives*, 676.

69. Sunder, *Bill Sublette, Mountain Man*, 110. According to an account by Robert Campbell, who was with Sublette and Sinclair, Sinclair was killed on the spot. Hardee, *Pierre's Hole!*, 210.

70. Hardee, *Pierre's Hole!*, 187–263.

Chapter 4

71. In his Report, Bonneville states that after building his cantonments on the Salmon River, he awaited the arrival of the rest of his men from their fall hunting and trapping. Irving, on the other hand, suggests Bonneville dispersed his parties before leaving for the Salmon River (Irving, *Three Western Narratives*, 695). Whatever the case, it's unlikely Bonneville would have waited until early November to send out his fall hunting parties.

72. See Irving's account of the chronology, chapters VIII–X, *Three Western Narratives*.

73. Lovell, *Benjamin Bonneville*, 58.

74. Hafen, *Mountain Men and Fur Traders of the Far West*, 279; Irving, *Three Western Narratives*, 700–01.

75. Irving, *Three Western Narratives*, 692.

76. Hardee, *Pierre's Hole!*, 295.

77. Irving, *Three Western Narratives*, 675.

78. Ibid, 688–89.

79. Historian Robert Utley states that "Bonneville and the men with him on the Salmon simply sat out the winter, trapping hardly at all." They may not have trapped much, but Bonneville stated clearly in his Report that he and his men left the cabins sometime after November 28 and then left the area of the Salmon River on December 25 in search of Mathieu's party. He did not return to the area of the Nez Perce until almost spring (Utley, *Life Wild and Perilous*, 169).

80. Gilbert, *Westering Man*, 113.

81. Irving, *Three Western Narratives*, 709.

82. Ibid., 696–97.

83. Ibid., 720.

84. Ibid., 730.

85. Chittenden, *American Fur Trade of the Far West*, 310–11.

86. Hafen, *Mountain Men and Fur Traders of the Far West*, 278–79.

87. Irving, *Three Western Narratives*, 952.

88. Lovell, *Benjamin Bonneville*, 64.

Chapter 5

89. Utley, *Life Wild and Perilous*, 169.

90. Gowans, *Rocky Mountain Rendezvous*, 777–78.

91. According to Edith Lovell, "from Bonneville's caches, Joe Walker set up a store in one of [the fort's] blockhouses, exchanging munitions, knives and ornaments for skins" (*Benjamin Bonneville*, 65). Also see the comments from Charles Larpenteur about arriving at the rendezvous on July 8 and finding some of Bonneville's men "in a small stockade" (Gowans, *Rocky Mountain Rendezvous*, 813).

92. Irving, *Three Western Narratives*, 761.

93. Chittenden, *American Fur Trade of the Far West*, 311.

94. Lovell, *Benjamin Bonneville*, 54, 101.

95. Irving, *Three Western Narratives*, 759.

96. Hafen, *Mountain Men and Fur Traders of the Far West*, 279.

97. Gowans, *Rocky Mountain Rendezvous*, 870–73.

98. Hafen, *Mountain Men and Fur Traders of the Far West*, 280n.

99. Irving, *Three Western Narratives*, 766.

100. Ibid., 876.

101. Leonard and Wagner, *Leonard's Narrative*, 158.

102. Irving, *Three Western Narratives*, 877–78.

103. Ibid., 877.

104. Leonard and Wagner, *Leonard's Narrative*, 158–59n.

105. Irving, *Three Western* Narratives, 886.

106. Morris, "Mountain Men and the Taking of California."

107. Lovell, *Benjamin Bonneville*, 67.

108. Irving, *Three Western Narratives*, 763.

109. "Wolf Attacks on People," *Yellowstone Insider*.

110. Irving, *Three Western Narratives*, 775.

111. Ibid., 775–76.

112. Hardee, *Pierre's Hole!*, 296.

113. Irving, *Three Western Narratives*, 778.
114. Quoted in McDonald, "History of Navigation on the Yellowstone River."
115. Irving, 790.
116. Lovell, *Benjamin Bonneville*, 72.
117. Wolf, "Bonneville's Foray," 93–104.
118. Lovell, *Benjamin Bonneville*, 97.

Epilogue

119. Lovell, *Benjamin Bonneville*, 91–96.
120. Neilson, "Captain Bonneville," 629–30.
121. Lovell, *Benjamin Bonneville*, 159.
122. Ibid., 248.
123. Neilson, "Captain Bonneville," 627.
124. Irving, *Three Western Narratives*, 948.

BIBLIOGRAPHY

Articles and Electronic Resources

Abel-Henderson, Anne H. "General B.L.E. Bonneville Letters Procured by Anne H. Abel-Henderson." *Washington Historical Quarterly* 18, no. 3 (1927), 207–30. https://journals.lib.washington.edu.

Barnhart, Bill. "National Register of Historic Places Inventory—Nomination Form: Fort Bonneville." National Park Service (December 19, 1969). https://npgallery.nps.gov.

"Bonneville folder #448," Oregon Historical Society. Portland State Research Library. https://ohs.org/research-and-library.

Carter, J.R., and A. Rice Green, "Floods in Wyoming: Magnitude and Frequency." United States Department of the Interior. Survey Circular (1963). https://pubs.usgs.gov/circ/0478/report.pdf.

Conner, Jett B. "Presidential Power: Thomas Paine, Thomas Jefferson and the Louisiana Purchase," *Journal of the American Revolution* (May 26, 2020). https://allthingsliberty.com.

Eddins, O. Ned. "Was Fort Bonneville Really Nonsense?" *Rocky Mountain Fur Trade Journal* 5 (2011): 21–33.

Gardner, Mark L. "Wagons on the Santa Fe Trail, 1822–1880." National Park Service. Santa Fe, NM: Department of the Interior, 1997. https://www.nps.gov.

Hannon, James, Jr. "'A Life Wild and Perilous': Death in the Far West Among Trappers and Traders." *Rocky Mountain Fur Trade Journal* 5 (2011): 58–69.

Martin, Jill E. "'The Greatest Evil' Interpretations of Indian Prohibition Laws, 1832–1953." *Great Plains Quarterly* (2003): 2432. https://digitalcommons.unl.edu/greatplainsquarterly.

McDonald, John Gordon. "History of Navigation on the Yellowstone River." Thesis, University of Montana, 1950. https://scholarworks.umt.edu.

Morris, Larry E. "Mountain Men and the Taking of California, 1845–1847." *Rocky Mountain Fur Trade Journal* 10 (2016): 94–121.

Neilson. Barry J. "Captain Bonneville," *Annals of Wyoming* 8, no. 1 (April 1932): 608–28. https://archive.org/details/annalsofwyom8141932wyom/page/608/mode/2up.

Oregon Encyclopedia. "Jedediah Strong Smith." Portland State University and the Oregon Historical Society, Portland. https://oregonencyclopedia.org.

Roberts, Phil. "The Oil Business in Wyoming." *Wyoming State Historical Society*, November 8, 2014. https://www.wyohistory.org.

Wolf, James R. "Bonneville's Foray: Exploring the Wind Rivers in 1833." *Annals of Wyoming* 63, no. 3 (Summer 1991).

"Wolf Attacks on People." *Yellowstone Insider*, May 3, 2009. https://yellowstoneinsider.com.

Books

Bagley, Will. *South Pass, Gateway to a Continent*. Norman: University of Oklahoma Press, 2014.

Baumer, Jr., William H. *Not All Warriors*. Edited by Bill Thayer. New York: Smith & Durrell, 1941.

Chittenden, Hiram M. *The American Fur Trade of the Far West*. New York: Francis P. Harper, 1918. E-book, Astoria Printing, 2018.

Clark, J.C.D. *Thomas Paine: Britain, America, & France in the Age of Enlightenment and Revolution*. New York: Oxford University Press, 2018.

Conner, Jett. *John Adams vs. Thomas Paine: Rival Plans for the Early Republic*. Yardley, PA: Westholme, 2018.

———. *Thomas Paine: A Brief History of the Times That Tried Men's Souls*. Denver, CO: Jett B. Conner, 2020.

DeVoto, Bernard. *Across the Wide Missouri*. Boston: Houghton-Mifflin, 1947.

Field, Matthew C. *Prairie and Mountain Sketches*. Edited by Kate L. Gregg and John Frances McDermott. Norman: University of Oklahoma Press, 1957.

Gilbert, Bil. *Westering Man: The Life of Joseph Walker*. Norman: University of Oklahoma Press, 1985.

Gowans, Fred. *Rocky Mountain Rendezvous: A History of the Fur Trade 1825–1840*. Layton, UT: Gibbs Smith, 2005. Kindle edition, 2008.

Graves, John. *Goodbye to a River*. New York: Alfred A. Knopf, 1983.

Hafen, LeRoy Reuben, ed. *Mountain Men and Fur Traders of the Far West: Eighteen Biographical Sketches*. Lincoln: University of Nebraska Press, Bison Book edition, 1982.

Hardee, Jim. *Pierre's Hole! The Fur Trade History of Teton Valley, Idaho*. Pinedale, WY: Sublette County Historical Society, 2010.

Hawke, David Freeman. *Paine*. New York: Harper & Row, 1974.

Irving, Washington. *Astoria, Or Anecdotes of an Enterprise beyond the Rocky Mountains*. Norman: University of Oklahoma Press, 1965.

———. *Three Western Narratives: A Tale of the Prairies, Astoria, the Adventures of Captain Bonneville*. New York: Library of America, 2004.

Josephy, Alvin M., Jr., ed. *The American Heritage Book of Indians*. New York: American Heritage Publishing, 1961.

Lavender, David. *The Rockies*. New York: Harper & Row, 1968.

Leonard, Zenas, and William F. Wagner. *Leonard's Narrative: Adventure of Zenas Leonard, Fur Trader and Trapper, 1831–1836*. Cleveland, OH: Burrows Brothers Company, 1904.

Lovell, Edith Haroldsen. *Benjamin Bonneville: Soldier of the American Frontier*. Bountiful, UT: Horizon Publishers, 1992.

McPhee, John. *Rising from the Plains*. New York: Farrar, Straus and Giroux, 1986.

Nelson, Craig. *Thomas Paine: Enlightenment, Revolution, and the Birth of Modern Nations*. New York: Penguin, 2006.

Paine, Thomas. *The Complete Writings of Thomas Paine*. 2 vols. Philip S. Foner, ed. New York: Citadel Press, 1969.

Restad, Hilde Eliassem. *American Exceptionalism: An Idea that Made a Nation and Remade the World*. London and New York: Routledge, 2015.

Sunder, John E. *Bill Sublette, Mountain Man*. Norman: University of Oklahoma Press, 1959.

Utley, Robert M. *A Life Wild and Perilous*. New York: Holt Paperbacks, 1998. Kindle edition, 2015.

INDEX

ABOUT THE AUTHOR

Jett B. Conner is professor of political science emeritus at Metropolitan State University of Denver. He received his PhD from the University of Colorado, Boulder, and was awarded a National Endowment of the Humanities Summer Fellowship at Princeton University, where he studied America's founding period. Jett is a contributor to the *Journal of the American Revolution* (www.allthingsliberty.com), where his book *John Adams vs. Thomas Paine: Rival Plans for the Early Republic* was selected for its annual series of JAR books. He lives in Denver with his wife, Rosemary, relishes his retirement and enjoys travel, especially wolf and grizzly watching in Yellowstone National Park.